Inside the Alamo

Inside the
ALAMO

JIM MURPHY

DELACORTE PRESS

PICTURE CREDITS

Amon Carter Museum, Fort Worth: vi

Benson Latin American Collection, University of Texas at Austin: 2, 52

Daughters of the Republic of Texas Library, San Antonio: 3, 21, 28, 53, 56, 61, 63, 64, 68, 76, 82, 84, 111

Drawing by Thom Ricks, University of Texas Institute of Texan Cultures at San Antonio: 4

Sketch by Seth Eastman, gift of the Pearl Brewing Company. McNay Art Museum, San Antonio: 5

Stephen L. Hardin and the artist, Gary Zaboly: 6-7

Texas State Library and Archives Commission, Austin: 8, 11, 24, 35, 41, 42, 54, 58, 60, 77, 78, 79, 87, 95, 102, 105, 109

Center for American History, University of Texas at Austin: 18, 22, 70, 88, 110

DeGolyer Library, Southern Methodist University, Dallas: 9, 26, 90, 92

William R. Chemerka and the artist, Gary Zaboly: 34

Gift of the Hoblitzelle Foundation. Kari and Esther Hoblitzelle Collection, Dallas Museum of Art: 36

Alan C. Huffines and the artist, Gary Zaboly: 15, 39, 44, 72

Collection of Western Americana, Beinecke Rare Book and Manuscript Library, Yale University, New Haven: 30, 100

Future bequest of Ms. Katharine Bradford. Long-term loan to the National Portrait Gallery, Smithsonian Institution, Washington, D.C.: 38

Department of the Navy: 49

Library of Congress, Washington, D.C.: 47, 85

San Antonio Conservation Society Foundation: 50

Texas State Preservation Board, Austin: 74, 96

San Jacinto Museum of History: 107

Gift of Robert L. B. Tobin in memory of Mr. and Mrs. John W. Todd. McNay Art Museum, San Antonio: 98

Gift of Ann Tobin in loving memory of Ethel Tobin Greenwald. McNay Art Museum, San Antonio: 99 top

Harry Ransom Humanities Research Center, University of Texas at Austin: 99 bottom

University of Texas Institute of Texan Cultures at San Antonio: 103

Published by
Delacorte Press
an imprint of
Random House Children's Books
a division of Random House, Inc.
1540 Broadway
New York, New York 10036

ools, visit us at

Library of Congress Cataloging-in-Publication Data
Murphy, Jim.
    Inside the Alamo/Jim Murphy.
      p. cm.
    Summary: An overview of the struggle between the Texan settlers and Mexico's General Santa Anna for control of Texas, with a detailed description of the 1836 siege of the Alamo. Includes biographical sketches and quotations of some of those involved.
    ISBN 0-385-32574-6 (trade) 0-385-90092-9 (lib. bdg.)
      1. Alamo (San Antonio, Tex.)—Siege, 1836—Juvenile literature.
2. San Antonio (Tex.)—History—Juvenile literature. [1. Alamo (San Antonio, Tex.)—Siege, 1836. 2. Texas—History—Revolution, 1835–1836.
3. Texas—History—Republic, 1836–1846.] I. Title.
F390.M86 2003
976.4'03—dc21   2002024029

The text of this book is set in 13.5-point Bell Monotype.
Book design by Trish Parcell Watts
Printed in the United States of America
April 2003
10 9 8 7 6 5 4 3 2 1
RRD

Contents

Main Plaza.

Alameda.

Alamo (1850).

Mission de la Concepcion.

SAN ANTONIO DE BEXAR.

Mission San José.

The New Bridge.

San Pedro Spring.

Mission San Juan.

A quiet morning in San Antonio de Béxar as painted by Hermann Lungkwitz in 1857.
This view was originally published in Germany as a way to entice German emigrants to the city.

CHAPTER ONE

"The Enemy Are in View!"

The town of San Antonio de Béxar lay silent and still. Most of its twenty-five hundred residents had already fled to the safety of ranches in the surrounding countryside, leaving behind just a handful of ordinary citizens. The other remaining inhabitants were soldiers of the Texan Army, tucked inside their rented houses and rooms, recovering from the previous night's *fandango*.

Suddenly, the grave stillness was shattered by the clanging warning bell, its harsh sound filling the air and racing along every twisting street, every narrow alley.

Grumbling and out of sorts, men stumbled outside to glare up at the bell tower of San Fernando Church. It was the second time that day that the bell had disturbed them and their pounding heads. They were

> A *FANDANGO* WAS A PARTY CONSISTING OF LIVELY DANCING, GAMBLING, AND A GREAT DEAL OF DRINKING.
> ⇌

ANGLO SETTLERS IN TEXAS WERE KNOWN AS TEXIANS OR TEXICANS. HISPANIC SETTLERS WERE CALLED TEJANOS. WHILE "TEXIAN" AND "TEXICAN" CONTINUED TO BE USED TO DESCRIBE THE INHABITANTS OF THE AREA UNTIL THE CIVIL WAR, THEY WERE GRADUALLY REPLACED BY "TEXAN" DURING THE 1840S.

in no mood for another false alarm. Moments later, reality jolted them alert.

"The enemy are in view!" the sentry in the bell tower was yelling. This was confirmed by one of their two commanders, twenty-six-year-old Lieutenant Colonel William Travis. The tall, lean Travis raced past, ordering the men to withdraw across the river to the crumbling mission-fortress known as the Alamo. It's very possible that Travis was accompanied by his twenty-two-year-old slave, a black man named Joe, carrying an armful of Travis's personal possessions and weapons.

It was February 23, 1836, and after weeks of rumors, the Mexican Army under the command of General Antonio López de Santa Anna had finally arrived. There was no secret about why Santa Anna was there: he had come to crush the Texan rebels—Texian and Tejano alike—and reclaim the vast territory of Texas for Mexico.

The soldiers in town grabbed up clothes, rifles, blankets, bits of food—anything that might come in handy and could be easily carried—before hurrying off to the fort. The thirty to thirty-four soldiers who had been wounded the previous December in the battle for Béxar either hobbled along as best they could or were carried in their beds.

This was no orderly retreat. These soldiers were almost all volunteers who hadn't drilled very much since driving the Mexican forces out of Béxar—and Texas—in December. They weren't big on military procedures, so they limped, ran, or were hauled to the Alamo in a hectic, every-man-for-himself manner.

Decked out in his formal uniform, Santa Anna seems to be studying viewers with a wary look.

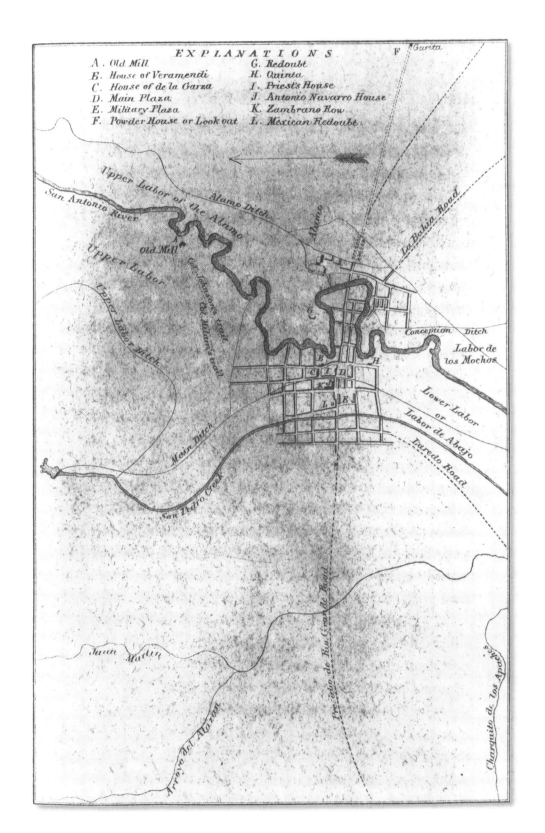

EXPLANATIONS.

A. Old Mill
B. House of Veramendi
C. House of de la Garza
D. Main Plaza
E. Military Plaza
F. Powder House or Look out

G. Redoubt
H. Quinta
I. Priest's House
J. Antonio Navarro House
K. Zambrano Row
L. Mexican Redoubt

An 1835 map of Béxar based on one drawn by John W. Smith just after the Alamo was captured in December (1835) from General Cós and his troops. Santa Anna's men entered the city via the Presidio de Rio Grande Road in the center.

Almost all the Tejano citizens still in town slammed and locked their doors, hoping the fight to come would be over quickly. Between twenty and thirty Tejanos were followers of a local rancher, Captain Juan Seguín, and rushed with him to join their Texian friends.

Accompanying all these soldiers were a number of women and children, though precisely how many is unclear. At least ten women and nine children would find shelter at the Alamo. They ranged in age from Alejo Perez, Jr., who was eleven months old, to Petra Gonzales, who was remembered as being "a very old woman."

As this stream of people neared the Alamo, they were met by others hurriedly leaving. Captain Philip Dimitt decided he did not like the fighting odds and was fleeing while he could, though he promised to send reinforcements. Also scampering off were Lieutenant Benjamin Nobles and a Béxar storekeeper, Nat Lewis.

Lewis had spent the morning taking inventory in his store. When the warning bell began clanging, he stuffed the most valuable items into saddlebags and scurried to the Alamo ahead of the crowd. But the wild disorder in the Alamo and the appearance of Mexican soldiers entering town were more than his nerves could stand. So Lewis shouldered his saddlebags and started walking east

One of Juan Seguín's men, Gregorio Esparza; his wife, Ana; and seven-year-old son, Enrique, flee Béxar with other citizens. Not pictured are Enrique's two younger brothers. Enrique later provided detailed and dramatic recollections about the siege of the Alamo.

across open country toward the town of Gonzales, seventy miles away. When asked later why he hadn't stayed at the Alamo, Lewis snapped defensively, "I am not a fighting man; I'm a businessman."

An interior view of houses in the Alamo (probably in the center of the long west wall), sketched in 1848 by Seth Eastman.

Colonel Jim Bowie, Travis's co-commander, also left the fort, though not to save his hide. Despite a severe illness that drained his body of energy, Bowie had pushed himself up from his sickbed at the sound of the warning bell. His first thought was to get his two sisters-in-law, Juana Alsbury and Gertrudis Navarro, and Juana's baby daughter to the safety of his room on the west wall of the Alamo. This accomplished, he gathered a small detachment of soldiers and went to hunt for food in a nearby shantytown known as La Villita. Bowie and his men spent the next forty-five minutes or so breaking down the doors of the deserted mud-and-stick huts called *jacales*. They eventually collected nearly ninety bushels of corn.

Meanwhile, other men had herded together some thirty head of cattle. These men were now whipping the cattle along toward the main gate, where there was soon a traffic jam of bellowing animals and noisy, agitated men, women, and children.

Within the Alamo the scene was just as chaotic. The sick were brought to the makeshift hospital Dr. Amos Pollard had assembled on

THERE WAS NO OFFICIAL UNIFORM FOR THE TEXAS ARMY. THE MEN IN THE ALAMO PROBABLY WORE A MIXTURE OF CIVILIAN CLOTHING AND BITS AND PIECES OF ARMY SURPLUS UNIFORMS. ONE UNIT, THE NEW ORLEANS GREYS, DID HAVE COMPLETE UNIFORMS. MANY OF THE TEJANOS WORE LOOSE-FITTING COTTON PANTS, COLORFUL VESTS, AND WIDE-BRIMMED SOMBREROS.

⚜ THE ALAMO ⚜

When it was built by Spanish missionaries in 1718, the Alamo was called the Mission of San Antonio de Valero. It came to be known as the Alamo after a company of Spanish soldiers from Alamo de Parras in Mexico stayed there in the 1790s.

The mission's main purpose was to convert local Native Americans to the Catholic religion and teach them to be hardworking, law-abiding laborers for their Spanish masters. This process was referred to as reducing, and it had worked very well in subjugating other native populations, such as the Aztecs and Incas. But it failed badly in Texas, where such powerful groups as the Comanches, the Caddos, and the Tonkawas refused to be dominated by Spanish civilization, religion, or military might.

The Alamo complex was little used over the years, and it took a terrible pounding in the December 1835 Battle of Béxar. As a result, its buildings were in disrepair. Great chunks of the adobe-and-limestone walls were missing, especially on the north side. The chapel was the sturdiest structure, with stonemasonry walls four feet thick and twenty-two and a half feet tall. Yet even this formidable building had a caved-in roof and mounds of debris in the interior.

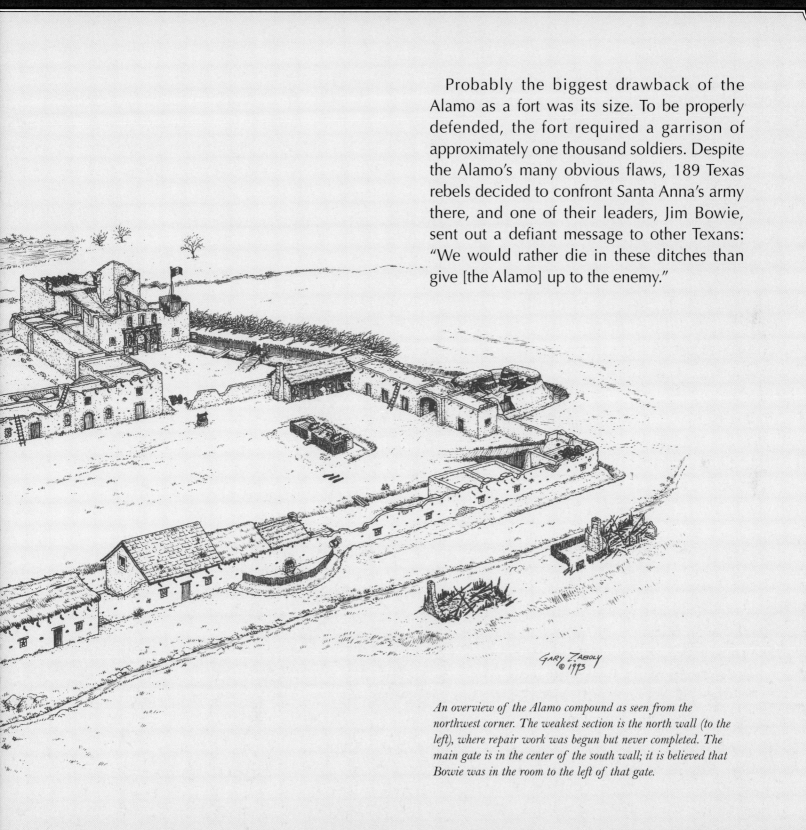

Probably the biggest drawback of the Alamo as a fort was its size. To be properly defended, the fort required a garrison of approximately one thousand soldiers. Despite the Alamo's many obvious flaws, 189 Texas rebels decided to confront Santa Anna's army there, and one of their leaders, Jim Bowie, sent out a defiant message to other Texans: "We would rather die in these ditches than give [the Alamo] up to the enemy."

GARY ZABOLY
© 1993

An overview of the Alamo compound as seen from the northwest corner. The weakest section is the north wall (to the left), where repair work was begun but never completed. The main gate is in the center of the south wall; it is believed that Bowie was in the room to the left of that gate.

the second floor of the long barracks. The women hurried their trembling children into the chapel and made themselves as comfortable as possible in its tiny, dark rooms.

A scattering of men had already mounted the walls and were passing a telescope from one to another and gesturing frantically as they counted enemy soldiers who were methodically searching houses in Béxar. Other Alamo soldiers were clambering up wobbly ladders, rifles in hand, calling out to ask what the enemy was doing. Barrels of powder were rolled up dirt ramps to waiting cannon while officers issued orders, men scurried about, and animals whinnied and snorted nervously.

The chief surgeon for the Alamo garrison was Dr. Amos Pollard.

"As I ran across the Main Plaza, I saw a splendid sight. A large army was coming toward me on horseback and on foot. They wore red coats and blue trousers with white bands crossed over their chests. Pennants were flying and swords sparkled in the bright winter sun."

ENRIQUE ESPARZA IN A 1907 ACCOUNT OF THE SIEGE
PUBLISHED IN THE *SAN ANTONIO EXPRESS*

The only person who seemed to know what he was doing was Sergeant William B. Ward. Ward was a notorious drunk and could usually be seen stumbling about on unsteady legs. Today he was cold sober and in complete control of himself, his crew, and the two cannon covering the inside of the main gate.

Finally, everyone pushed inside and the gates to the Alamo were closed and barred. Approximately 157 men, plus the 19 or so women and children, were inside, waiting, watching, and worrying.

They were a varied lot, these Alamo defenders. They came from all over the United States—from Terrapin Creek, Kentucky; Hurricane

THE ALAMO GARRISON HAD AN ESTIMATED 816 RIFLES, MUSKETS, PISTOLS, AND SHOTGUNS WITH THEM WHEN THE SIEGE BEGAN.

Township, Missouri; Avon, New York; Athens, Georgia; and Cedar Springs, Pennsylvania. Several had journeyed from England, Ireland, Scotland, or Denmark. The talk of what the enemy might do next was a rich mixture of tongue-twisting brogues and other accents—flinty New England, soft southern, and lilting Spanish.

Only a handful of the defenders were true frontiersmen or soldiers used to hardship and handling a rifle. The vast majority had more traditional occupations; among them were lawyers, doctors, teachers, and farmers. Lewis Duel had been a Manhattan plasterer, Charles Zanco a housepainter, George Kimball a hatter. William Garnett, a Baptist preacher, rubbed shoulders with hard-drinking, fast-talking, tobacco-chewing Henry Warnell, a professional jockey. Sixteen teenagers would eventually enter the Alamo, the youngest a fifteen-year-old named William Philip King. And one of the most famous men in all America, David Crockett, was there too.

An etching of David Crockett based on an 1834 painting by John G. Chapman. Crockett is wearing a simple cloth hunting outfit and a flat-crowned, broad-brimmed hat, not the legendary buckskins and coonskin cap.

It would be difficult to assemble a group that had so little in common and yet shared a single belief so passionately. Each man felt to his bones that Texas was not only his home but also his destiny. These men considered the land—and the economic benefits it promised—theirs, and they were willing to fight to hold on to it.

The remarkable thing was how quickly this spirit of unity had developed and taken hold. Before 1820, hardly any Anglo-Americans lived in the vast territory known as Texas. Of course, not many Mexicans called it home either—fewer than three thousand citizens occupied the three major towns of La Bahía, Nacogdoches, and Béxar.

Mexico had been trying to settle Texas with its own people for nearly three hundred years with little success. Mexicans simply refused to move there, considering the lands beyond the Rio Grande nothing more than a desolate desert filled with savage Native American tribes. As late as 1833, Mexicans living just south of Texas dismissed it as being "out of the world."

The Mexican government was so desperate to settle the land that in 1820 it came to an unusual (and some Mexicans said foolish) decision. Foreigners—including those from Mexico's northern neighbor, the United States—would be allowed to settle in Texas. There were several legal provisions for settlement, but the most important was that newcomers had to become Mexican citizens and swear allegiance to that country.

The invitation worked better than anyone in the Mexican government had anticipated. In December 1821, Stephen Austin brought a small band of settlers to an area near the Brazos River. Despite the harsh terrain, the sometimes harsh climate, and the frequent attacks by Native American tribes, the colony of San Felipe flourished. After this success, other colonies took root.

"I must say as to what I have seen of Texas, it is the garden spot of the world. The best land and the best prospects for health I ever saw, and I do believe it is a fortune to any man to come here. There is a world of country to settle."

DAVID CROCKETT IN A LETTER TO HIS FAMILY, JANUARY 8, 1836

People in the United States began hearing excited reports about Texas and its promise. Vast lands could be had for little money; the soil was excellent in places, and certain crops—such as cotton— would grow well there; endless grasslands could nourish a huge number of cattle. By 1830, more than sixteen thousand Anglo-

❧ STEPHEN AUSTIN ❧

The settlement of Texas by Anglo-Americans was initiated by Moses Austin in 1821 when he received permission to bring three hundred families into the region. Moses died before his plan could be carried out, but his son, Stephen, took over and later that year established a colony at what would eventually become San Felipe de Austin.

Stephen Austin was a skillful advocate for his settlers. When Mexico won its independence from Spain in 1821, Austin was able to negotiate an extension to his land grant from the new government. Nine years after that, the Mexican government prohibited Anglo immigration, but Austin won a special exemption for his colony. Eventually, he would bring more than fifteen hundred families into Texas.

Austin was a strong believer in cooperating with the government south of the Texas border, and in every way he was a loyal Mexican citizen. Even after Santa Anna seized control and established himself as clearly anti-American, Austin urged negotiations, not war. Most Texians agreed with Austin and considered themselves members of what came to be called the Peace Party, which Stephen Austin led.

In 1833, Austin journeyed to Mexico City to petition Santa Anna for independent statehood for Texas under Mexican rule. A small but very vocal group known as the War Party had arisen in Texas, and they wanted complete independence from Mexico. Austin's trip was designed in part to counter this group's growing popularity. His request was denied, though Santa Anna did make several important concessions, such as allowing jury trials.

But as Austin headed home, Santa Anna had him arrested because he suspected that Austin was urging the people of Texas to rebel. Austin would remain in a Mexico City jail for eighteen months. He emerged a changed man and in September 1835 urged war on Mexico proclaiming, "Every man in Texas is called upon to take up arms in defence of his country and his rights. . . ."

Stephen F. Austin, known as the Father of Texas.

Americans had built homes, plowed fields, and established businesses in Texas.

Of course, these people didn't forget the things they believed in because they had moved to a new country. Most of these Anglo-Americans brought along a feeling that they and their children had certain rights that could not be taken from them by any government: freedom of speech, freedom to carry on their businesses with as little government interference as possible, the right to a fair and open trial, the right to be represented when laws and taxes were imposed.

For the most part, these Anglo settlers were content to live under the terms imposed by Mexico for immigration. There were, however, specific things about their relationship with Mexico that troubled them and left them wary.

The Mexican constitution adopted in 1824 joined the Texas province with another, creating the State of Coahuila y Texas. Almost all this new state's representatives came from Coahuila, and none of them were Anglo. What is more, the constitution did not provide for the election of local or state officials. The federal government in Mexico City chose each state's governor, and the governor appointed the local mayors, the *alcaldes*, who ran each town. Simply put, local citizens had little or no say in who represented them. Finally, there was no guarantee of a jury trial open to the public.

Despite these problems, most settlers in Texas were still willing to accept Mexican authority. Stephen Austin declared firmly in 1830, "I consider that I owe *fidelity & gratitude to Mexico. That* has been my motto, & I have impressed it upon my Colonists."

In fact, it was the Mexican government that was most upset over the situation in Texas. Two separate reports, one by General Manuel Mier y Terán and the other by a civilian inspector, José María Sánchez, worried that the rapid increase in the Anglo population would soon obliterate Spanish culture in Texas. In addition, Terán's report listed a series of abuses that needed to be stopped. Settlers were refusing to pay taxes, even though they had agreed to do so when they swore allegiance to Mexico. Plantation owners ignored the government's stand against slavery, while merchants were smuggling large amounts of goods to avoid tariffs.

To halt further growth in the Anglo population, the Mexican government passed a law in 1830 that in effect banned U.S. citizens from settling in Mexican territory. To enforce this new law, Mexican troops began arriving in Texas in 1831.

These moves further alienated the Anglo settlers; they were convinced that they would never be accepted as genuine Mexican citizens and that they would always be viewed as potentially dangerous. This feeling was surprisingly accurate. Sánchez's report referred to the Anglos as "our enemies from the North" and suggested they had a "treacherous design" to break free of Mexican rule.

Santa Anna made a bad situation worse after he became Mexico's president in 1833. He took office pledging that each state of Mexico, including Texas, would have the power to make its own laws and dispense justice. But behind the backs of the Mexican legislature, he began concentrating power in his own hands. One year later, he took complete control of Mexico, dismissing all federal, state, and local representatives. Eventually, he would do away with the Mexican republic completely by suspending the Constitution of 1824.

Anglo settlers had left the United States in favor of a different country. Now that country had, in their eyes, abandoned them. No longer citizens of the United States, no longer citizens of Mexico, they were Texans.

THE FIRST ARMED CLASH OF THE REVOLUTION OCCURRED AT ANÁHUAC IN JUNE 1835. THAT WAS WHEN TWENTY-FIVE REBELS LED BY WILLIAM BARRET TRAVIS FACED OFF AGAINST THE MEXICAN SOLDIERS GARRISONED THERE AND FORCED THEM TO SURRENDER. THE VAST MAJORITY OF PEOPLE IN TEXAS WERE OFFENDED BY THIS ACT OF AGGRESSION AND FORCED TRAVIS TO APOLOGIZE TO MEXICAN AUTHORITIES.

What is considered the first battle of the Texas War of Independence took place at Gonzales on October 2, 1835—fourteen years after Stephen Austin brought the first legal Anglo settlers to the region, and just five years after the enactment of the anti-immigration laws. By December 1835, Mexican troops and Mexican rule had been driven out of Texas.

But now Santa Anna was back and ready to reclaim Texas as part of his Mexico.

The Alamo defenders saw squadron after squadron of Mexican soldiers march into town, accompanied by the deep roll of military drums and the dry creak of field carriages hauling cannon. Sixteen hundred Mexican troops would occupy Béxar that day, with another four thousand on the way. Then, as the shadows darkened in the short winter afternoon, those inside the Alamo saw a chilling sight.

"The President with all his staff advanced to Campo Santo (burying ground). The enemy . . . fled and possession was taken of Béxar without firing a shot."
COLONEL JUAN ALMONTE IN HIS DIARY

Mexican soldiers raced up the stairs to the bell tower of San Fernando Church. Within minutes they were able to carry out one of Santa Anna's first orders on retaking Béxar. They hoisted a large bloodred banner plainly visible from the Alamo eight hundred yards away. The banner was the traditional symbol that no mercy would be shown the enemy.

The banner was meant to scare the rebels, to force them to surrender and then plead for their lives. But instead of giving up, the emotional Travis ordered the biggest cannon in the fort fired as a defiant answer. The eighteen-pounder roared, its thunderous boom echoing for miles around.

In response, Santa Anna had a howitzer lob grenades into the Alamo compound. One, two, three, four exploded, scattering metal shards in all directions but injuring nobody.

The Mexicans would have continued firing, but a rider emerged from the Alamo carrying a white flag of truce. The men inside the Alamo were willing to fight, and they certainly understood that they could die doing so. But they weren't fools bent on suicide; they knew perfectly well that their small force couldn't hold out very long once the rest of Santa Anna's troops arrived.

That is why first one, then a second messenger went out from the Alamo with a note for Santa Anna. Each note asked whether the Mexicans had requested a meeting. It's possible that the Alamo defenders really thought the enemy wanted a parley to negotiate the surrender of the Texan soldiers; it's also possible that the notes were a ploy to get negotiations started without having to say directly that they were willing to surrender.

Whatever the reason, both messages were harshly rejected by Santa Anna's aide-de-camp, Colonel José Batres: "... The Mexican army cannot come to terms under any conditions with rebellious foreigners to whom there is no other recourse left ... than to place themselves immediately at the disposal

The bloodred banner being attached to the metal cross atop the bell tower of San Fernando Church. The skull and crossbones depicted here are from a banner drawn by Captain José Juan Sánchez Navarro in his plan of the Alamo siege. Mexican soldiers and artillery have marched through the main plaza and are already searching the town. The Alamo is in the distant background.

❧ Who's in Charge Here? ❧

There was probably never a rebellion as poorly organized as the one that took place in Texas in 1835–36. Before the outbreak of fighting, Texas was divided into two political factions. The Peace Party, headed by Stephen Austin and including Jim Bowie, urged citizens to remain loyal to Mexico and its laws. The War Party, whose members included such prominent citizens as Henry Smith, Ben Milan, Sam Houston, and William Travis, stood for complete independence from Mexico.

Most citizens backed Austin's position. Even after Austin was released from his Mexican prison in 1835 and declared, "War is our only recourse," division remained. To establish a unified provisional government, a Consultation of All Texas was called to meet in San Felipe in November 1835. It managed to name Henry Smith as president of the republic, as well as a fifteen-member council that included one representative from each municipality in Texas. But true unity eluded them.

Within weeks, Smith and the council were feuding openly and calling each other names. Eventually, the council impeached Smith, then fired him (though it had no authority to do so) and appointed a new governor. Smith retaliated by dismissing the council (something he likewise had no authority to do), threatened to shoot council members on sight, and proceeded to carry on a one-man government.

The split had profound consequences, especially when it came to moving ahead with the rebellion militarily. Both Smith and the council commissioned officers and appointed commanders for the regular and volunteer armies. But whom should the soldiers follow and obey?

It seemed that anyone who could rally a group of men around him could push aside an appointed commander and take charge. Jim Bowie did this a number of times. He went to the Alamo with instructions from Sam Houston to blow up the structure and get the remaining troops and artillery to a safe location. He decided to ignore those orders. Then, after the commander of the Alamo specifically appointed Travis to lead the troops while he went home, Bowie seized control anyway.

Knowing that time to prepare for Santa Anna was growing desperately short, Bowie and Travis eventually worked out an uneasy joint command. But the rest of Texas floundered along, squabbling over who had power. Officers frequently asked for leaves of absence or resigned their commissions when upset, while soldiers up and left if they did not agree with officers. In the end, those at the Alamo were left to take care of themselves.

of the Supreme Government from whom alone they may expect clemency. . . ."

The Alamo defenders knew perfectly well whom the phrase "Supreme Government" referred to: Santa Anna. Those inside the Alamo knew also that Santa Anna could be ruthless with his enemies. Less than a year before, he had crushed a rebellion in the Mexican state of Zacatecas with brutal efficiency, killing thousands of rebels and innocent civilians.

So instead of putting their lives in the hands of such a man, the Alamo defenders chose to sit tight, hoping that reinforcements would arrive in a day or two.

"The rebels saw that . . . there could be no hope for a peaceful understanding and that they had no other way but to conquer, die or abandon the fruits and labors of their fondest dreams."

GENERAL VICENTE FILISOLA IN HIS MEMOIRS

Miles away on the open prairie, the distant boom of the eighteen-pounder startled two men and made them turn in the direction of the fort. Dr. John Sutherland and John W. Smith had both been ordered by Travis to carry urgent dispatches to the citizens of Gonzales. The one Sutherland carried was brief, almost breathless in its urgency: "To any of the inhabitants of Texas," it began. "The enemy in large force is in sight. We want men and provisions. Send them to us. We have 150 men and are determined to defend the Alamo to the last. Give us assistance."

It was one of many cries for help that would go out from the Alamo in the days to come.

Even in old age, the eyes of Enrique Esparza reflect the horror he witnessed as a boy during the siege of the Alamo.

CHAPTER TWO

"In This War There Are No Prisoners"

After the first wave of Mexican soldiers had secured Béxar, their commander-in-chief rode in on horseback, trailed by his staff officers. Santa Anna was a regal-looking man of forty-two with polished boots and a crisply pressed uniform heavy with gold edging. Buckled to his side was a gleaming silver-and-gold sword that had cost seven thousand dollars.

"Riding in front [of the soldiers] was Santa Anna, El Presidente*! This man was every inch a leader . . . I was very impressed."*

ENRIQUE ESPARZA IN A 1907 NEWSPAPER ACCOUNT

THE MEXICAN ARMY CAREFULLY MEASURED EACH SOLDIER'S HEIGHT. THEY AVERAGED BETWEEN FIVE AND FIVE AND A HALF FEET TALL. SANTA ANNA WAS ONE OF THE TALLEST SOLDIERS IN THE ARMY, AT FIVE FEET TEN INCHES.

Santa Anna and his staff went through the military plaza and past San Fernando Church, at last arriving at the house of the Yturri family on the north side of the main plaza. It was a squat little structure, humble in appearance but solidly built. Santa Anna decided it would serve nicely as his headquarters and reined in his horse.

He should have been elated. The rebel forces in Béxar had given his soldiers little opposition. In fact, the enemy had scampered from town like whipped dogs and were now cowering in the crumbling adobe mission. Yet Santa Anna was anything but happy.

For one thing, the bulk of his troops were nowhere in sight. The moment he had heard that settlers in Texas had taken up arms against his troops, he had put together an army of sixty-five hundred men and marched from Mexico City. Santa Anna was an avid student of French emperor Napoleon Bonaparte's military strategies and styled himself the Napoleon of the West. One of Napoleon's tenets was "A rapid march augments the morale of an army and increases its means of victory."

Santa Anna's aim was to surprise the rebels by arriving in late winter. The weather would be terrible, and there would be no grass for the animals. No sensible commander would stage a march during this part of the year—which was precisely what Santa Anna hoped the rebels would believe, and precisely what they did believe. Repeated warnings that the Mexican Army was on the way did little to motivate those at the Alamo to prepare for battle. Just the night before, they had celebrated George Washington's birthday with an all-night party of drinking and dancing.

Unfortunately, Santa Anna's passion for speed meant that he, too, failed to prepare adequately. He had not brought along enough food, water, tents, blankets, or medical supplies for his troops. Only one doctor accompanied the entire army, and he turned out to be a quack.

Worse, a great many of the men under Santa Anna's command—anywhere from a thousand to two thousand—were completely untrained or even unfit to be soldiers. As soon as the army headed north, the line of march began to stretch out as inexperienced men grew exhausted. Hundreds died in the dry, hot hills of Coahuila; hundreds more perished in Texas when a savage blizzard caught them by surprise; hundreds more deserted rather than risk death. Without enough forage, the oxen hauling wagons and cannon weakened and had to be prodded forward with bayonets.

Santa Anna set up his headquarters in the Yturri house, the low building to the left of the Plaza House.

"It broke one's heart to see all this, especially many women with children in their arms, almost dying of thirst, crying for water. The tears that they were shedding were all that they could give them to drink."

GENERAL VICENTE FILISOLA IN HIS MEMOIRS

Adding to Santa Anna's annoyance, the two large siege cannon that could punch holes in the frail walls of the Alamo were only now arriving at the Texas border, some two hundred miles away. It would take at least two weeks for them to be dragged over that distance.

All these military problems were annoying, and the commander-in-chief did nothing to hide his anger as he tossed the reins of his horse to an aide and stalked into the Yturri house. But what really made his blood boil were the rebels themselves.

Santa Anna's forced march north took him and his troops through harsh terrain similar to this winding mountain road near the mouth of Zacate Creek.

These ungrateful foreigners had been invited to set up homes in the province of Texas by the Republic of Mexico. For just thirty dollars, each settler received 4,428 acres of land on which he could live tax free for ten years. Little was asked in return for such generosity. Settlers had only to obey a few rules. Slavery was forbidden, and newcomers were required to join the Catholic Church, in name at least. They had to become citizens of Mexico and swear an oath of allegiance to the government.

Santa Anna had disapproved of this settlement plan from the start, but he was a mere army officer when the plan went into effect and could do nothing to stop it. Quite simply, he bristled at the idea of giving Mexican land to foreigners and did not trust them to keep their promises.

Almost immediately he saw that he was correct about the Anglos. A number of the immigrants violated the laws by buying up hundreds of claims. One of the rebels inside the Alamo, Jim Bowie, had amassed more than seven hundred thousand acres of land in his first two years in Texas. In addition, Americans by the thousands poured across the border illegally and did not bother to practice the Catholic religion; others smuggled in goods or brought in slaves.

To Santa Anna these immigrants weren't settlers. They were greedy invaders.

What is more, they were arrogant. The rebels had dared to attack Mexican troops at Gonzales, Goliad, and the old Concepción mission in October 1835. The most humiliating Mexican loss had come in December 1835 there in Béxar. That was when a Mexican force of fifteen hundred well-trained, well-equipped soldiers under the command of General Martín Perfecto de Cós—Santa Anna's own brother-in-law—had been driven from the Alamo and Texas by just three hundred settlers.

LOST IN THIS FIGHT FOR TEXAS WERE THE PEOPLE WHO FIRST OCCUPIED THE LAND: NATIVE AMERICANS. BEFORE EUROPEANS ARRIVED, THE POPULATION IN NORTH AND SOUTH AMERICA IS ESTIMATED TO HAVE RANGED FROM 70 MILLION TO MORE THAN 100 MILLION. DEADLY DISEASES BROUGHT OVER BY EUROPEANS, SUCH AS SMALLPOX, MEASLES, AND TYPHOID, QUICKLY DECIMATED THESE PEOPLE. HOWEVER, DESPITE THE DRAMATIC LOSS OF POPULATION, THERE WERE STILL MORE THAN 140 FUNCTIONING TRIBES IN TEXAS IN 1700.

BUT THE END OF THESE NATIVE AMERICAN NATIONS WAS AT HAND. DISEASE AND WARFARE FURTHER DEPLETED THEIR NUMBERS. YET EVIDENCE OF THEIR PRESENCE LINGERED. EVEN THE NAME TEXAS COMES FROM THEIR LANGUAGE. NATIVE AMERICANS GREETED THE EXPLORERS WHO WERE THERE TO TAKE THEIR LAND WITH THE WORDS *TECHAS! TECHAS!*, WHICH MEANS "FRIENDS! FRIENDS!"

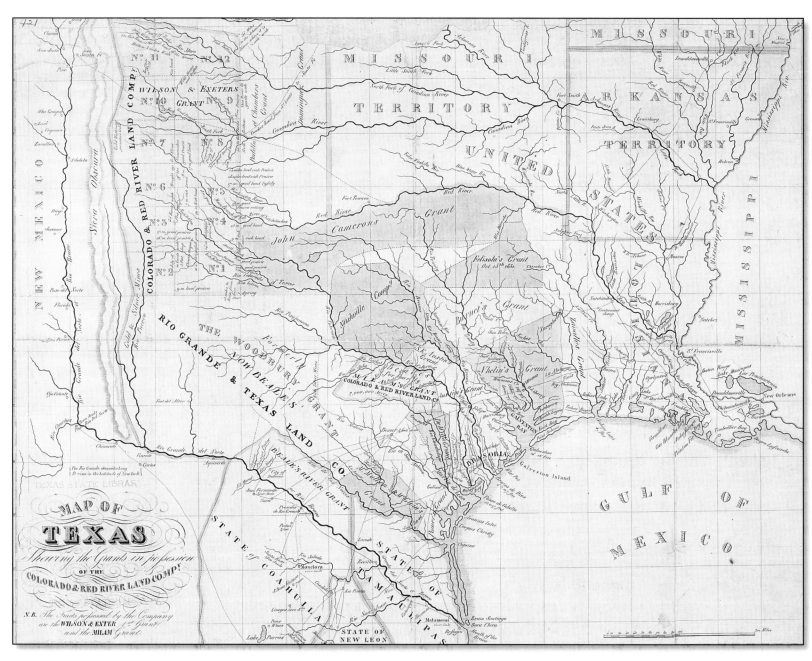

Individuals often sold their parcels of land to enterprising people like Jim Bowie, or to financially powerful companies. This map shows the millions of acres of territory purchased by the Colorado and Red River Land Company, the Rio Grande and Texas Land Company, and others.

To add to the insult, the rebels had not even bothered to prepare for Santa Anna and his army. Béxar citizens acting as spies brought him frequent reports about the lazy foreigners. How they idled away their days and did very little to strengthen the mission-fort. How they danced and drank at night. They even dared to fly the flag of the Mexican republic, the government Santa Anna had abolished when he was finally able to sieze power.

"The superiority of the Mexican soldier over the mountaineers of Kentucky and the hunters of Missouri is well known. Veterans seasoned by twenty years of wars can't be intimidated by the presence of an army ignorant of the art of war, incapable of discipline, and renowned for insubordination."

DECREE BY JOSÉ MARÍA TORNEL, MEXICAN MINISTER OF WAR

As he set up his command headquarters on February 23, Santa Anna had a number of options in his campaign to retake Texas. The most prudent would be to camp in Béxar for a week or so to allow more troops to arrive. He could then assign a small force to contain those inside the Alamo and starve them into submission. This would leave him free to strike at other rebel strongholds with the rest of his army.

But Santa Anna chose to stay and deal with the Alamo himself.

His official reason for remaining in Béxar was that the town could be used as a supply station for his troops as they purged Texas of rebels. A more likely reason had to do with who was inside the mission-fort.

His spies had told him that several important leaders of the revolution were there: Jim Bowie, for one, and the loudmouthed William Travis. And a new one, the one everybody called Crockett. Santa Anna did not know much about David Crockett, but he did know that the

A pencil sketch of William Barret Travis by Wiley Martin in December 1835.

man was famous in the United States and that he had entered Mexican territory illegally. Defeating all three of these men would draw attention to Santa Anna and his formidable army and do much to crush the spirit of rebellion.

The commander-in-chief knew from personal experience how to deal with Anglo rebels. Twenty-three years earlier, in 1813, a ragtag army of 850 Anglos from the United States had invaded Texas and joined up with 600 or so Mexican residents near the border. They had marched south, taking one town after another until they reached Béxar. A few miles outside town, near the Medina River, they clashed with Mexican military forces and were routed. Most of the Anglos not killed in battle were captured and executed; then their bodies were hung by the heels from tree branches. The few who survived took the hint and fled to the safety of the United States.

Santa Anna was a young lieutenant at the Battle of Medina when he saw firsthand how force and intimidation could be used to control rebellion. A similar victory was required over these new invaders inside the Alamo. They had to be exterminated to teach rebels in other Texas towns (as well as those in the United States who wanted to seize Mexican land) to fear him and his army. "[Texas] should be razed to the ground," Santa Anna told his staff, "so that this immense desert . . . might serve as a wall between Mexico and the United States."

Filled as he was with an intense hatred of the Anglo foreigners, Santa

Anna's first official order was to have the bloodred banner raised high on San Fernando Church. "I neither ask for nor give quarter," he said when questioned about his policy of no mercy. *"En esta guerra sabe vd. que no hay prisioneros."* ("As you know, in this war there are no prisoners.")

"Don Santa Anna, feeling as every true Mexican ought, the disgrace thus sustained by [Mexico], is making every preparation to wipe out the stain in the blood of those perfidious foreigners."
TAMAULIPAS GAZETTE, OCTOBER 1835

But instead of begging for mercy, the insolent rebels once again defied him, this time with a blast from a cannon. Then, one after the other, they sent out two men under white flags of truce to see what sort of surrender terms might be offered.

The idea that these foreign rebels thought they could negotiate with him as an equal further incensed Santa Anna. He was, after all, the head of the Mexican government, the government the Anglo settlers had pledged to obey in all matters. They had only two choices: they could surrender unconditionally or they could fight.

Santa Anna then set about preparing his army for what was to come.

For officers squeamish about executing prisoners, he quoted Mexican law: "Foreigners invading the republic . . . shall be judged and treated as pirates." All Anglos were included in this condemnation, even those who had entered Texas legally. Mexican rebels were also included. Santa Anna's reasoning was that "any Mexican guilty of the crime of joining these adventurers loses the rights of a citizen." As such, there was no need for a trial, no need for mercy; the death sentence could be carried out immediately. Having wrapped his no-mercy policy in the law, he added, "An example is necessary."

❖ SANTA ANNA ❖

History books are filled with villains, but Santa Anna certainly ranks as one of the most hated, even by his own countrymen. He was a greedy man, a political genius, a vain and arrogant fool, a good soldier, a great Mexican patriot, a cruel and cowardly commander, and an opium addict.

Santa Anna was a complicated man with many faults, but indecisiveness was not one of them. When he heard that rebels in Texas were threatening Mexican authority, he assembled a formidable army in a matter of weeks, then force-marched it across six hundred miles of inhospitable and largely uninhabited terrain. Soldiers and officers suffered horribly along the way, as did the nearly fifteen hundred women and children who accompanied them. But Santa Anna did not relent and had his army in Texas with astonishing speed.

He was just as unrelenting when he ordered that captured rebel soldiers be exterminated.

As a young cadet, Santa Anna had taken part in the Battle of Medina in 1813. After the Mexican Army defeated the rebels, most of the Anglo survivors were executed and their bodies hung by the heels from tree branches. The impressionable young Santa Anna saw how quickly the rebellion evaporated after this and learned a valuable lesson: harsh measures worked. He was determined to apply that lesson to these new rebels.

A great many officers and soldiers in the Mexican Army were honorable men who had come to Texas to fight what they saw as a legitimate threat to their country. Unfortunately, Santa Anna's personality, actions, and words were so extreme and cruel that they completely overshadowed the reason the Mexican forces had marched on Texas, as well as the many heroic actions of his soldiers and officers.

Santa Anna, again in formal uniform, but this time sporting a mustache. Some people think he has a more sinister and suspicious appearance in this picture than in the one that appears in the first chapter.

"We have mentioned earlier that the commander in chief had already brought upon himself the ill will of the army. The hatred for him was found even among his friends and intimates."

LIEUTENANT JOSÉ DE LA PEÑA IN HIS MEMOIRS

As for the common soldiers of his army, Santa Anna knew they were frustrated and grumbling and growing angrier every day. They were angry with him for making them take part in the campaign, angry with their officers for pushing them on day after painful day, angry with a God who would send them so many plagues—disease, hunger, thirst, snow, and rain—before even a single shot had been fired.

Santa Anna sensed this growing tension, and as any good commander would, he directed it at the rebels. In a rousing proclamation, he praised his men for their bravery and then told them of their enemy's contempt for them as warriors. "Wretches! They will soon learn their folly," he thundered, adding as encouragement: "Soldiers, our comrades have been shamefully sacrificed at Anáhuac, Goliad, and Béxar. . . . You are those destined to punish these murderers."

> OF THE FIFTEEN HUNDRED *SOLDADERAS* WHO SET OUT FOR TEXAS, ONLY THREE HUNDRED MADE IT TO BÉXAR. THERE ARE NO RELIABLE ESTIMATES OF THE NUMBER OF CHILDREN WHO DIED DURING THE MARCH.
>
>

TO THE CITIZENS OF TEXAS.

———— ✳ ————

COMMANDANCY OF THE ALAMO, BEJAR, FEB. 24, 1836.

FELLOW-CITIZENS,

I am besieged by a thousond or more of the Mexicans, under Santa Ana. I have sustained a continual bombardment and cannonade, for twenty-four hours, and have not lost one man. The enemy have demanded a surrender at discretion, otherwise the garrison is to be put to the sword, if the fort is taken. I have answered the demand with a cannon shot, and our flag still waves proudly from the walls. *I shall never surrender nor retreat:* then I call on you, in the name of liberty, of patriotism, and of every thing dear to the American character, to come to our aid, with all possible despatch. The enemy are receiving reinforcements daily, and will, no doubt, increase to three or four thousands, in four or five days. Though this call may be neglected, I am determined to sustain myself as long as possible, and die like a soldier who never forgets what is due to his own honor and that of his country.

VICTORY OR DEATH.

W. BARRET TRAVIS,
Lieutenant-Colonel Commandant.

P. S. The Lord is on our side. When the enemy appeared in sight, we had not three bushels of corn; we have since found, in deserted houses, eighty or ninety bushels, and got into the walls twenty or thirty head of beeves.   T.

Travis's "Victory or Death" letter is considered one of the most patriotic in our nation's history. This broadside poster of it was displayed throughout Texas shortly after Governor Henry Smith received it.

CHAPTER THREE

"I Hope Help Comes Soon"

When the sun came up on February 24, the Alamo defenders found Mexican soldiers already hard at work. In town, out of the range of Texan rifles some four hundred yards away, Santa Anna's men were digging a trench to accommodate three cannon.

Inside the Alamo another crisis developed. After weeks of illness, Jim Bowie collapsed completely and was so weak that he could not even lift his head from his pillow.

Bowie had ridden into Béxar on January 19 in seeming health. The commander of the Texan Army, General Sam Houston, had ordered him there to blow up the Alamo and haul away its twenty-one cannon.

> IN 1860, ONE OF THE EARLIEST ALAMO HISTORIANS, CAPTAIN REUBEN POTTER, STATED THAT JIM BOWIE'S HEALTH HAD WORSENED BECAUSE OF AN ACCIDENT THAT HAPPENED WHILE THE ALAMO WAS BEING READIED FOR ATTACK. POTTER LATER ADMITTED THAT THIS STATEMENT WAS NOT ACCURATE.

Despite the dilapidated condition of the fort and the extremely low morale of the men, Bowie did not carry out his orders.

Bowie, along with the then commander of the Alamo, Lieutenant Colonel James C. Neill, believed that the Alamo occupied a key position. Not only was it the first fortification the enemy would encounter on entering Texas, it was also ideal as a supply base for whichever army controlled it. The structure needed a great deal of repair work and the men had to be whipped into fighting shape, but both tasks seemed possible.

Obviously Bowie was in good health—or at least good enough health—to make this decision. He had the energy to visit acquaintances and friends in Béxar to arrange for supplies, and to negotiate a loan to pay the soldiers. He also had the stamina to drink and socialize through many nights.

Granted, not much work was done to prepare the Alamo for attack, a lapse for which Bowie has been sharply criticized by historians. He—and everyone else involved in the Texas Revolution—assumed that Santa Anna wouldn't arrive until new grass was growing in the spring. Bowie was able, though, to win the loyalty of the troops and rekindle in them a sense of purpose.

Bowie was still reasonably strong when twenty-six-year-old Lieutenant Colonel William Travis arrived on February 2. Travis was inexperienced, headstrong, and egotistical. He also believed in maintaining strict military discipline at all times, especially when it came to following orders immediately and without question. Before Lieutenant Colonel Neill went home to care for his sick family, he appointed Travis commander of all the Alamo troops.

Bowie wouldn't stand for this arrangement. Not only was he older than Travis, he'd had much more actual experience in battle. So Jim

Bowie began issuing commands and acting as if he were the only commander. And when Travis insisted that an election be held, the men overwhelmingly chose the genial Bowie to be their leader.

All this took a great deal of energy, so Bowie's illness had clearly not yet progressed to the point of incapacitating him. Bowie was also clearheaded enough to realize that a disgruntled Travis could divide the troops. So he and Travis worked out a way to share command of the Alamo.

It isn't clear what Bowie's illness was. Dr. John Sutherland said only that Bowie had "a disease of a peculiar nature, not to be cured by an ordinary course of treatment." Historians have suggested tuberculosis, pneumonia, typhoid fever, and typhoid pneumonia as the culprit. The truth is that we will probably never know for certain what finally stopped Jim Bowie.

> *"Bowie was dying—dying slowly. He had been sick a long time, had lost considerable flesh, and now was a hulk of a man. He coughed almost incessantly, agonizingly. His pulse was rapid. He had fever. His breath was short, quick."*
>
> ANDREA CASTAÑON RAMÍREZ DE VILLANUEVA, BETTER KNOWN AS MADAME CANDELARIA

We do know that after Bowie collapsed on the second day of the siege, he moved out of the room he was sharing with Gertrudis and Juana and her baby. He was taken to another room in the low barracks next to the main gate, probably because he worried he might be contagious. His physical decline was so rapid and so complete that he never left his cot again, though on two or three occasions he had his bed carried outdoors to visit with Juana, Gertrudis, and other friends. His last official acts as commander were to turn over responsibility for the Alamo and its

> EVEN THOUGH SCOUTING REPORTS CLEARLY STATED THAT THE MEXICAN ARMY WAS APPROACHING, SAM HOUSTON, THE COMMANDER OF THE TEXAS ARMY, ASKED THE ACTING GOVERNOR FOR AND RECEIVED A ONE-MONTH FURLOUGH FROM DUTY AT THE END OF JANUARY.

NORTH WALL DIGGERS UNDER FIRE.

GARY ZABOLY © 96

As the Alamo defenders worked on the north wall, they were frequently interrupted by enemy artillery fire. Some of the projectiles fired were solid iron balls meant to punch holes in the walls of a fort. Others, like this one, had fuses and powder inside and were designed to explode, injuring and killing enemy solders with flying bits of metal.

DURING THE THIRTEEN-DAY SIEGE, THE MEXICANS FIRED APPROXIMATELY 335 SOLID CANNONBALLS AT THE WALLS OF THE ALAMO, AND ANOTHER 86 ROUNDS OF EXPLODING SHELLS.

troops to Travis and to ask the men to support the young commander.

Bowie's military involvement in the siege was over. But even confined to bed, he still exerted a strong emotional influence over the troops. The majority of the men had committed themselves to stay and defend the Alamo solely because of Jim Bowie. As Isaac Millsaps said in a letter to his wife, "Col. Bowie is down sick and had to be to bed [but] he is still ready to fight. . . . He tells us help will be here soon & it makes us feel good."

The loss of Bowie's official leadership shook the men terribly, but they seem to have accepted the situation and Travis's command readily. They may have seen the need for his by-the-book approach now that they were being confronted by hundreds of enemy soldiers.

Immediately, Travis set the garrison to work on strengthening the walls of the Alamo. Dust rose in billowing clouds as men hurriedly dug trenches inside the main plaza and added new artillery positions around the walls. They also dug a well to supplement the trickle of water that entered the fort through an irrigation ditch.

The north wall was in particular need of attention. Before Santa Anna had arrived, the Alamo troops had managed to patch a large hole in that wall with logs six inches thick. Now they began tossing up dirt against the logs. Military standards at the time indicated that the wall required at least one and a half feet of packed dirt to stop a musket ball and from eight and a half to ten feet to withstand bombardment from a cannon.

⇒ JIM BOWIE ⇐

Jim Bowie may have ridden to Béxar on orders from Sam Houston, but he was no mere messenger boy. Standing six feet tall, with sandy hair, Bowie was a strong-willed individual who believed in himself and his ability to make decisions on his own.

He had grown up in the tough sugar-cane region of Louisiana, where, as one historian put it, "he led a wild childhood, full of roping wild deer, trapping bear, breaking mustangs, even riding alligators." He was a noted and feared fighter and was especially handy with the big knife he always carried.

As he grew older, he took this vast supply of energy, determination, and ego and applied it to making his fortune—first in the slave trade and then in the sale of fraudulent land grants in Louisiana and Arkansas. In 1828, when he was in his early thirties, he ended up in Texas and quickly made a fortune in land speculation.

Bowie was obviously no saint, but he wasn't a frontier lout either. He was well educated and could speak and write French and Spanish as well as English. He rarely raised his voice, was cool and deliberate at all times, and was extremely generous to his friends.

Bowie was unusual among Texians because he genuinely appreciated the culture and ways of the Mexican people. He bought a house in Béxar, embraced Mexican culture, and married nineteen-year-old Ursula de Veramendi, whose father was the vice governor of the province.

His affection for the Mexican people continued even after Ursula and her parents died in a cholera epidemic in 1833. In fact, Jim Bowie's desire to protect his friends and relatives in Béxar may have contributed to his decision to disobey Houston's order to blow up the Alamo.

This portrait shows Jim Bowie as he looked during a trip to the East Coast between 1831 and 1834.

Andrea Castañon Ramírez de Villanueva, better known as Madame Candelaria, as she appeared in an 1891 painting by William Henry Huddle.

MANY HISTORIANS DISMISS MADAME CANDELARIA AS A COMPLETE FRAUD. SHE WAS A RESIDENT OF BÉXAR AND A NOTED *CURANDERA*, OR FOLK HEALER, WHO USED NATIVE AMERICAN REMEDIES AND HERBS TO CARE FOR THE SICK. WHILE SHE CERTAINLY INVENTED A GREAT DEAL OF ALAMO "HISTORY," IT IS VERY POSSIBLE SHE WAS CALLED IN TO ADVISE ON BOWIE'S CARE.

"The Mexicans have shown imbecility and want of skill in this Fortress as they have done in all things else. . . . Taking into consideration the scarcity of tools we have done well in mounting and remounting Guns and other necessary work."

MAJOR GREEN B. JAMESON IN A LETTER TO GOVERNOR HENRY SMITH

The feverish work was made more difficult on the afternoon of February 24 when the Mexicans' first cannon battery was completed and opened fire. Every so often the hard work inside the Alamo was interrupted as a shell soared over the wall and exploded in the plaza.

Those not part of these work crews lined the fort's five hundred yards of wall, watching and waiting. Because high-quality powder was in such short supply, Travis had ordered his troops to hold their fire unless the Mexicans launched an attack. His one extravagant use of powder was to have the eighteen-pounder fired three times a day, morning, noon, and night, as a signal to those in the countryside that the Alamo was still holding out. The Mexicans launched a few probing assaults, but not much else disrupted the mind-numbing routine of the Alamo defenders.

When not on watch or patching up the fort, the men had little to do but cook and eat their meals, chat, and sleep (usually at their posts or very near them). Small groups were assigned various tasks, such as getting and distributing water and slaughtering and cutting up steer. But such chores didn't use up much of the day and didn't take the men's minds off the two most important questions nagging at them: when would Santa Anna attack, and would reinforcements arrive in time?

The women of the Alamo settled in as best they could and created a daily routine to keep themselves and the children as busy as possible. Some helped care for the thirty to thirty-four injured and ill men in the hospital. It is also believed that at least one additional woman, identified as Madame Candelaria, might have been called in to help minister to Jim Bowie's medical needs. Most women prepared food for their husbands, children, and a few soldiers, mended and cleaned clothing, and did a variety of other necessary chores. A great deal of time was absorbed in taking care of and playing with the nine children under the age of twelve. Still, being confined in the small rooms of the chapel and having their sleep constantly interrupted by enemy cannon fire must have been both exhausting and terrifying.

The spirits of those within the Alamo were further tested when the weather deteriorated on the third night of the siege. An icy wind pushed the temperature down near freezing, and a week of cold, drizzly days followed. Men huddled around small fires for warmth, talked, whittled, and did whatever else they could to pass the hours.

The troops were fortunate in one respect: David Crockett was there to entertain them. He was a born storyteller who could take the simplest incident and spin it into an elaborate and involving yarn. It might be about growing up in the wilds of Tennessee, hunting bear as a young boy, or meeting people in Washington, D.C., where he had served as a U.S. congressman. On several occasions he even staged musical duels with a twenty-eight-year-old Scot named John McGregor. With Crockett on fiddle and McGregor on bagpipes, the two would battle to see who could make the most noise, while the men, women, and children applauded and shouted encouragement.

Such diversions helped a little, but they couldn't hide the truth of the situation. Every day more and more Mexican troops entered Béxar, hundreds of them at a time. Isaac Millsaps observed the increasing number of bright red-and-blue uniforms and said, "I hope help comes soon cause we can't fight them all."

STRANGERS ON THE STREET AND ALL THE NEWSPAPERS CALLED HIM DAVY (OR DAVEY) CROCKETT, BUT HE PREFERRED TO BE CALLED DAVID. CROCKETT SIGNED ON AS A PRIVATE IN THE TEXAS ARMY IN JANUARY 1836 AND BECAME A PART OF CAPTAIN WILLIAM HARRISON'S COMPANY, KNOWN AS THE TENNESSEE MOUNTED VOLUNTEERS. WHILE CROCKETT NEVER BECAME AN OFFICER, HE WAS RECOGNIZED AS AN INFORMAL LEADER OF THE "TENNESSEE BOYS" AND GIVEN THE HONORIFIC "COLONEL."

✷ DAVID CROCKETT ✷

If ever there was a person who was truly larger than life, it was David Crockett. He left home in 1798 when he was twelve years old and quickly became an accomplished woodsman, hunter, and trapper. He had little formal education (less than six months' worth) but was considered an intelligent, if somewhat lazy, student. "When a man can grin and fight," he said on several occasions, "or whip his weight in wildcats, what is the use of reading and writing?"

His greatest gifts were a natural talent for leadership and an ability to charm anyone within hearing distance with a humorous story. His ready wit and open, engaging personality won him many followers and led him into a political career that lasted seventeen years and included three terms in Congress. In the end, however, his naïve approach to Washington politics (he challenged President Andrew Jackson openly and repeatedly on a number of issues, including the harsh treatment of Native Americans by U.S. troops) led to his losing a bitterly contested election for a fourth term in office in 1835.

He left Tennessee in a huff after this loss, telling the citizens, "You may all go to hell and I will go to Texas." His journey south was covered by the newspapers as if it were a triumphant royal procession with speeches and parties all along the way. When he arrived in Béxar on February 8, 1836, everyone in town and in the Alamo poured out to meet the famous David Crockett and hear him give a speech. By this time, Crockett was a wholehearted supporter of the Texas rebellion, able to proclaim: "I have come to aid you all that I can in your noble cause."

A formal David Crockett dressed in his city clothes, painted by Chester Harding in 1834.

Oddly enough, people came and went from the fort freely throughout most of the siege. During lulls in the bombardment, townspeople wandered between the lines without trouble. Madame Candelaria might have been one such visitor. Captain Juan Seguín had his meals brought in, and one resident of Béxar, Margarito García, made frequent nighttime visits to the Alamo to chat with friends.

Santa Anna could have shut off access to the fort, but he decided not to during the early days of the siege. He knew that some of Béxar's Tejano residents would bring valuable information to his enemies, but he also knew that in the same way he could find out about the rebels:

Inside the Alamo on a cold, bleak day.

how well armed they were, how much food and ammunition they had. He might have sealed off the Alamo sooner if he had known what Travis was up to.

During the siege, sixteen couriers galloped out of the Alamo, streaked through the Mexican lines, and raced across the Texas countryside. Launcelot Smither headed out on the twenty-third of February to tell the citizens of Gonzales that the Mexican Army had arrived; Robert Brown went out on or just after the twenty-fifth with pleas for help; Juan Seguín also left on the twenty-fifth, headed for Gonzales; James Bonham was dispatched on the twenty-seventh with an urgent plea for Colonel James Fannin in Goliad. One after the other, some by night, others by day, they carried Travis's reports about the Alamo garrison to the people of Texas and to the world beyond.

When compared to men like Bowie and Crockett, William Barret Travis was a virtual unknown before the siege. He had come to Texas from Alabama in 1831 after a failed marriage and opened a law practice.

From the start Travis was an avid and vocal supporter of Texas's independence from Mexico. Once the rebellion began, Travis sulked because he was hardly involved in the battles that eventually drove the Mexicans out of Texas at the end of 1835. He was made a lieutenant and then a captain, given a tiny squad of men, and sent out into the prairie to burn grassland the Mexicans might use for forage. He was kept far away from camp in part because he wasn't well liked.

> TRAVIS WAS SO LITTLE KNOWN THAT WHEN WORD OF THE ALAMO APPEARED IN NEW YORK NEWSPAPERS, HE WAS CALLED TRAVERS, WHILE IN NEW ORLEANS HE WAS REFERRED TO AS FRAVERS.

"[Travis] was very ambitious. He hungered and thirsted for fame—not the kind of fame which satisfies the ambition of the duelist and desperado, but the exalted fame which crowns the doer of great deeds in a good cause."

JONATHAN KUYKENDALL, FRIEND OF TRAVIS

❧ WILLIAM BARRET TRAVIS ❧

William Travis was a lawyer, a lieutenant colonel in the Regular Texas Army, and Alamo garrison co-commander all by the time he was twenty-six. He was also a young man filled with idealism, anger, and ambition. He considered himself a leader of men, though his oversized ego and petulant behavior often rubbed those men the wrong way. While traveling to the Alamo in January 1836, for instance, nine of his thirty-nine men became fed up enough with his antics to desert.

Like many self-centered individuals, Travis rarely criticized his own conduct. In a letter to the governor of Texas about the desertions, Travis lamented that the "volunteers can no longer be relied upon," and then threatened to resign: "Sir, I am unwilling to risk my reputation (which is ever dear to a volunteer) by going off into the enemy's country with so little means, so few men, and these so badly equipped. . . ."

When Travis felt he was in the right, he could dig in his heels and be as stubborn as anyone. From the moment he entered Texas in 1831, he was a vocal member of the War Party, a group who wanted to break free of Mexican rule and set up an independent country. Fueling his resolve was his belief that Mexicans were an inferior race and should not be allowed to rule over Anglos. Never mind that the vast majority of people in Texas were content to live peacefully under Mexican rule, wanted to negotiate a fair way to do so, and contemptuously referred to Travis and others like him as war dogs. For Travis, war was the only answer.

Travis brought all this angry determination to his decision making as Alamo co-commander. Once Santa Anna had taken away any hope of an honorable surrender, Travis had only two choices. He and the garrison could attempt to flee—but running away was not particularly honorable. The other choice was to stand and fight. Travis, ever the war dog, chose to fight.

Travis has a thoughtful, sad expression in this portrait by Henry Arthur McArdle. Travis had ordered a very fancy uniform from the prestigious New Orleans tailors McKinney & Williams, but it doesn't seem to have arrived before the Alamo fell. Sergeant Felix Nuñez took Travis's coat after the battle and said it was made of homemade Texas jean.

Travis was subsequently made a lieutenant colonel, but this wasn't enough for him. He felt he deserved a bigger command with more responsibility, and when it did not come his way, he threatened to resign. Travis would do this three times before he found himself bottled up at the Alamo.

It was here, at last, that his real talents shone. For despite his faults—and he had many—Travis did not lack courage, and he had a real flair for inspirational writing. So he spent a great deal of time during the siege in his small office dashing off one emotion-filled patriotic message after another.

He was not above exaggerating for effect or even changing events around altogether. The purpose of these messages was to get help for his besieged command, and he would do or say just about anything to achieve this.

His letters were at times anxiously hopeful—"I have every reason to apprehend an attack from [Santa Anna's] whole force very soon; but I shall hold out to the last extremity, hoping to secure reinforcement"—and at other times downright angry—"If my countrymen do not rally to my relief, I am determined to perish in the defense of this place, and my bones shall reproach my country for her neglect."

But Travis's letters are remembered most for their bold assertion of freedom and the way they urged Texans to declare independence and carry on the fight despite the overwhelming odds. One such missive went to the delegates who were then assembling in Washington-on-the-Brazos to decide whether to proclaim Texas a separate nation. "Let the Convention go on," he advised them, "and make a declaration of independence; and we will understand, and the world will understand what we are fighting for. . . . Under the flag of independence, we are ready to peril our lives a hundred times a day, and dare the monster who is fighting under a bloodred flag, threatening to murder all prisoners and make Texas a waste desert."

On the eighth day of the siege, March 1, it seemed as if Travis's pleas for help had indeed been heard. That night a band of thirty-two men and boys slipped through the Mexican lines and entered the Alamo. They were from Gonzales, and the brave little group was officially dubbed the Gonzales Ranging Company of Mounted Volunteers. Today, they are remembered as the Immortal Thirty-two.

Spirits inside the Alamo soared. Surely if the Gonzales troops had responded, other reinforcements would soon follow. They were especially certain that Colonel Fannin would appear with the four hundred soldiers he had at Goliad, just two days away. Other Texans would also arrive, rifles in hand. Soon, those inside the Alamo speculated, the horizon would be dotted with hundreds of fellow freedom fighters ready to take on the Mexicans.

TRAVIS'S "VICTORY OR DEATH" LETTER LEFT BÉXAR ON FEBRUARY 24. IT ARRIVED IN SAN FELIPE THREE DAYS LATER AND MADE IT TO THE COASTAL TOWN OF VELASCO ON MARCH 4. SHIPS CARRYING COPIES OF THE LETTER REACHED NEW ORLEANS ON MARCH 16 AND NEW YORK ON MARCH 30, FINALLY ARRIVING IN BOSTON DURING THE FIRST WEEK OF APRIL.

AS THE MEN FROM GONZALES APPROACHED THE ALAMO IN THE DARK, A SENTRY ON THE WALL FIRED AT THEM AND HIT ONE MAN IN THE FOOT. THERE IS SPECULATION THAT ON OR AROUND MARCH 3, ANOTHER RELIEF FORCE OF SIXTY MEN MAY HAVE ARRIVED FROM SAN FELIPE. THIS WOULD BRING THE TOTAL ALAMO GARRISON TO APPROXIMATELY 250. TO DATE, HOWEVER, THERE IS NO PROOF THAT THIS SECOND RELIEF FORCE EXISTED OR ARRIVED.

Exploding shells from several locations rain on the Alamo defenders, sending hot metal and pieces of stone flying in every direction.

CHAPTER FOUR

"The Alamo Must Fall"

Santa Anna focused all his intense energy and hatred on laying siege to the Alamo. His actions were guided by a French military strategist named Sebastien Le Prestre de Vauban. Vauban was not in Béxar with the Mexican Army; in fact, he had died in 1707. But his tactics for attacking a fortress were still being used widely in the nineteenth century. More important, Santa Anna's hero, Napoleon, had followed Vauban's strategies with remarkable success. What was good for Napoleon was certainly good enough for his avid student.

Vauban believed that no fort was impregnable. All an attacker had to do was develop a detailed plan intended to reduce the fort's ability to resist. First, the fort had to be surrounded and sealed off, so that reinforcements and supplies (especially food and powder) could not be brought in. Next, a series of steadily advancing trenches had to be dug to allow artillery and soldiers to be moved closer and closer to the walls of the fort.

"Up until now they have shown themselves contemptuous, confident of the strong position that they maintain, and basing their hopes upon the great resources of their colonies and of the United States of the North. However, they shall soon be finally disillusioned."

SANTA ANNA IN A DISPATCH TO JOSÉ MARÍA TORNEL, MEXICAN MINISTER OF WAR

Cannon fire day and night would deprive defenders of sleep and sap their will to fight, while dwindling food supplies would wear them down even further. Eventually, artillery would be close enough to pound the fort's walls to dust and bring its starving occupants into submission. If for some reason the fort still resisted, an infantry assault could be launched from the trenches.

"At evening the music struck up, and went to entertain the enemy with it and some grenades."

COLONEL JUAN ALMONTE IN HIS DIARY

Santa Anna was personally involved in every detail of his siege. He helped position artillery and direct the movement of troops. When the first battery of cannon opened fire on February 24, Santa Anna was there to observe the event.

The commander-in-chief was far too preoccupied with details that should have been left to junior officers. On the second day of the siege a supply of two thousand pairs of shoes arrived from Mexico, and

Santa Anna was on hand to supervise their distribution to his troops.

Even his officers worried that Santa Anna was overextending himself. Lieutenant Colonel José Juan Sánchez Navarro confessed his nervousness in his diary: "His Excellency himself attends to all matters whether important or most trivial. I am astonished to see that he had . . . assumed the authority of major general . . . of quartermaster, of commissary, of brigadier generals, of colonels, of captains, and even of corporals. . . ."

"What will become of the army and the nation if the Most Excellent President should die? Confusion and more confusion because only His Excellency knows the springs by means of which these masses of men called the army are moved."

CAPTAIN JOSÉ JUAN SÁNCHEZ NAVARRO IN HIS DIARY

Aged and in failing health, President Andrew Jackson was still a formidable champion of American expansion to the West.

Why this obsession with detail? Santa Anna felt that Mexico's honor and his own were on the line. He had boldly and publicly predicted that the Alamo would fall in the early days of March and that the rebellion in Texas would be over soon thereafter. He was also worried that the United States might send troops into Texas to help out the Texian settlers.

This was no idle worry on Santa Anna's part. President Andrew Jackson was a noted expansionist intent on settling as much of the North American continent as possible with U.S. citizens. He had offered to purchase Texas for five million dollars in 1829 and cautioned Mexico that it should accept the offer to avoid "collisions" with the United States. The deal had been turned down, but it was clear that the United States still had its eye not just on Texas but on all Mexican territory to the west.

What is more, as soon as word of the Texas rebellion reached him in late 1835, Jackson ordered the Sixth Regiment of the U.S. Army to assemble along the Mexican-U.S. border at the Sabine River. News of these troops was reported in the *New Orleans Bee* and was quickly relayed to the Mexican government and Santa Anna.

Finally, the officer in charge of the Sixth Regiment was General Edmund P. Gaines, a man with a personal interest in seeing Texas break away from Mexico. His cousin, James Gaines, was a resident of Texas and was at that moment helping to draft a declaration of independence at Washington-on-the-Brazos. All of these things made Santa Anna impatient to defeat the rebels and reestablish legal and military control over Texas.

During the opening days of the siege, Mexican soldiers dug more and more ditches for the placement of cannon—one on Powder House Hill to the southeast, another along the Alamo ditch to the northeast, yet another due north, and another to the west. In all, nine cannon were eventually blasting away at every corner of the fort.

Every so often, the bombardment would cease and a probing assault on the fort would be launched. These maneuvers were another tactic of Vauban's. They let the attackers see weak and strong points of the fort's defenses, and they forced the defenders to stay constantly alert and on edge.

These probing attacks followed a fairly predictable routine. Between twenty and thirty soldiers would venture out, staying low and getting as close to the Alamo as possible. They would retreat as soon as the rifle and cannon fire from the enemy became too intense or actually wounded one of their brethren. But on the twenty-fifth, Santa Anna had a surprise in store for the Alamo defenders.

THE MEXICANS MARCHED NORTH WITH TWENTY-ONE PIECES OF ARTILLERY, BUT ONLY NINE WERE IN PLACE AT ANY ONE TIME DURING THE SIEGE. WHILE ESTIMATES VARY WIDELY, IT IS NOW BELIEVED THAT THE ALAMO GARRISON HAD TWENTY-ONE PIECES, INCLUDING AN UNUSUAL NINE-INCH *PEDRERO* GUN USED TO FIRE STONES.

Occasionally Mexican troops would test the Alamo defenses by rushing them. This N. C. Wyeth painting depicts a handful of defenders responding with several volleys of fire.

At ten o'clock in the morning, Mexican soldiers were spotted approaching the San Antonio River. That day, however, instead of a mere handful of men, the landscape was swarming with them. In a matter of minutes, nearly three hundred soldiers splashed across the river and occupied houses in La Villita. Soon they were edging closer to the fort, dodging among adobe huts and wooden shacks.

A jacale, *a common type of home found in Béxar at the time of the siege.*

The alarm was shouted in the Alamo and the walls came alive with riflemen, though no shots were fired because they didn't yet have a clear view of the advancing soldiers. Eventually, the Mexicans broke into the open just ninety yards from the fort. At this point, the Alamo cannon began blasting away, sending thousands of hot metal shards into the faces of the enemy. The walls erupted with deadly rifle fire as well.

The Mexican soldiers in La Villita returned fire, but those out in the open broke ranks and began falling back, dragging their wounded with them. An intense battle followed, with artillery booming and rifles cracking from both sides while a thick cloud of smoke and excited shouts filled the air.

Once they had pulled back to cover, the Mexican soldiers were able to regroup and fire in a more orderly fashion. It was clear that if they held on, reinforcements could be brought in and a battery of artillery established in the shantytown.

Suddenly, the main gate of the Alamo flew open and Robert Brown, Charles Despallier, James Rose, and several others hurried out, torches in hand. With lead flying all around them, these men raced to the nearest huts and began setting them on fire. The ancient huts with their dry wood and thatched roofs were soon a crackling inferno. Flames began leaping from house to house. With the first few homes consumed in flames and enemy shot pouring in, the Mexicans finally lost heart at around noon and withdrew to the rear of La Villita.

Even though the Mexicans were still in the village, the Alamo defenders saw the fight as a clear victory and were jubilant. They had not just repulsed the enemy's attack; they had sent him running in disarray, killing two and seriously wounding six others. "I take great pleasure in stating," Travis would report in a letter to Sam Houston, "that both officers and men conducted themselves with firmness and bravery." He also added, "The Hon. David Crockett was seen at all points, animating the men to do their duty. . . ."

The Mexicans were impressed with the way the Alamo defenders handled themselves and their weapons and never again launched a major probing assault. One of their officers, Lieutenant José Enrique de la Peña, noted, "The reputation Texans have for marksmanship is well deserved."

Although the siege was being carried out as planned and every day more and more of his army arrived at Béxar, Santa Anna was becoming impatient. If anything, his eagerness to crush the Alamo was mounting.

FOR FASTER FIRING, MANY MEN INSIDE THE ALAMO KEPT FOUR OR FIVE LOADED RIFLES BY THEIR SIDES. MOST MEXICAN SOLDIERS CARRIED A BROWN BESS SMOOTHBORE MUSKET, PURCHASED FROM THE BRITISH AFTER THE NAPOLEONIC WARS. EACH WEIGHED JUST UNDER TEN POUNDS, WAS ACCURATE TO A DISTANCE OF ONLY TWO HUNDRED FEET, AND REQUIRED A COMPLICATED NINETEEN-STEP PROCEDURE TO LOAD.

For in addition to the hated rebels, he had General Juan José Urrea on his mind.

Earlier in the campaign, Santa Anna had ordered General Urrea east toward the Gulf of Mexico with six hundred men. He was to march along the coast and then head up the San Antonio River toward Goliad, where Colonel James Fannin and his 450 men were stationed in Fort Defiance. The plan called for Santa Anna to take the Alamo, then head to Goliad, where he and General Urrea could cut off the fort from front and rear.

General José Urrea was a highly skilled commander whose succession of victories in Texas stole much of Santa Anna's thunder. Urrea also opposed Santa Anna's policy of no quarter.

"Attention! Civil Wars are always bloody. Our soldiers ever aspire to shed the blood of foreigners who seek to take away from us our rights and menace our independence. This war is righteous, and should be without remorse."

DECREE BY JOSÉ MARÍA TORNEL, MEXICAN MINISTER OF WAR

The problem was that Urrea was moving very quickly, easily sweeping all resistance out of his path. When Santa Anna heard that his general had defeated one band of rebels at San Patricio on February 27 and another at Agua Dulce Creek on March 2, he fumed. It was clear that Urrea would assault Goliad long before he would. "Urrea does everything," Lieutenant de la Peña heard his commander-in-chief mutter. "He alone has the glory, while we just sit watching his victories."

Santa Anna's vanity simply could not allow that to happen. Especially since all that stood in his way was a miserable excuse for a fort and fewer than two hundred ill-mannered foreigners.

He began sending out increasingly angry messages to his second-in-command, General Vicente Filisola, who was in charge of the troops who had not yet reached Béxar. "Speed up the march," Santa

Anna commanded in one; "Send ahead all supplies you can gather," he urged in another. "Hurry the money held by the Commissary General." "Be sure to send up two or three hundredweight of salt, none here—not a grain—and we need it badly."

His impatience to be done with the Alamo soon prompted him to action. In the early evening of March 4, Santa Anna called a meeting of his generals. After some discussion, the commander-in-chief announced that the Alamo was to be stormed on the morning of March 6.

Some officers urged him to wait for more troops, or at least to wait until the two big twelve-pounders arrived. The cannon were now only two days away, and they could blow the fort's walls to shreds.

No, Santa Anna said. The assault could not wait. A band of rebel reinforcements had already slipped through Mexican lines and gotten into the Alamo. And he had heard rumors that a number of Texas towns were beginning to mobilize soldiers and that Colonel Fannin at Goliad might make an attempt to rescue the Alamo.

Forty-two-year-old Micajah Autry loads his rifle as he is about to take aim at Santa Anna.

"I go the whole Hog in the cause of Texas. I expect to help them gain their independence and also to form their civil government, for it is worth risking many lives for. From what I have seen and learned from others there is not so fair a portion of the earth's surface warmed by the sun."

MICAJAH AUTRY IN A LETTER TO HIS WIFE

✳ JAMES FANNIN ✳

Colonel James W. Fannin was the commander of the Texas forces at Goliad when he received an urgent message from Travis and Bowie that the Mexican Army had arrived in Béxar. "In this extremity," their message stated, "we hope you will send us all the men you can spare promptly." As if to shame Fannin into immediate action, the final line said, "We deem it unnecessary to repeat to a brave officer, who knows his duty, that we call on him for assistance."

Fannin had about 450 men with him, the largest single group of rebel soldiers in all Texas. It was natural that those at the Alamo would call on him for help. Yet Fannin never came to their aid.

He had legitimate reasons for not trying to rescue Béxar. He felt that his fort at Goliad was just as vital as the Alamo and did not want to leave it unprotected. And he did not think his troops were properly equipped or trained for battle. But most likely it was his own lack of confidence that stopped him. "I *feel*, I *know*," he wrote to the governor just days before the Alamo siege began, "that I am incompetent. . . . I do most earnestly ask of you, and any *real friend*, to relieve me. . . ."

Fannin made one attempt to take three hundred men and four cannon to the Alamo, but abandoned the effort after going a mile or so. He then retreated to his own fort and ignored all further pleas from the Alamo. He did fire off a lame explanation about his failure to rescue the Alamo, citing a lack of food and proper equipment. In the end, he wrote his own sad epitaph: "What must be the feelings of the volunteers now shut in Béxar? Will not curses be heaped on the heads of the sluggards who remained at home?"

A portrait of Colonel James Walker Fannin by Charles B. Normann. The commander of the forces at Goliad earned a questionable place in Texas history by failing to aid those besieged at the Alamo.

Several officers pointed out that without the big guns to soften up the enemy's defenses, many Mexican soldiers would die needlessly. Santa Anna answered this by holding up the leg of a chicken he'd had for dinner. "What are the lives of soldiers more than so many chickens?" he asked. "I tell you, the Alamo must fall, and my orders must be obeyed at all hazards."

Questions also arose again concerning the commander-in-chief's order of no mercy for prisoners. Many of his generals were deeply offended by the brutality of such a policy and did not think it would help quell the revolution. Napoleon had taken prisoners, they argued, and even Vauban had suggested that captives could be used as valuable bargaining chips.

His order stood, Santa Anna insisted, and he even instructed an aide to pistol-whip him if he himself wavered from the policy. As if to reinforce his intentions, a second bloodred banner was raised over Powder House Hill to the east. There it seemed to glow in the setting sun, clearly visible to his enemy.

When questioned later about the wisdom of killing survivors, Santa Anna dismissed the concerns with a quip. "If you execute your enemies," he told his staff, "it saves you the trouble of having to forgive them."

AFTER DEFEATING MEXICAN GENERAL CÓS AND HIS TROOPS AT THE ALAMO IN DECEMBER 1835, THE TEXAS ARMY FACED A DECISION: SHOULD THEY HOLD THE SOLDIERS PRISONER, FREE THEM, OR EXECUTE THEM? AFTER A HEATED ARGUMENT, CÓS AND HIS MEN WERE FREED AND EVEN PROVIDED WITH WEAPONS AND AMMUNITION SO THAT THEY COULD DEFEND THEMSELVES AGAINST BANDS OF COMANCHES.

James Butler Bonham returns to the Alamo in this imaginative 1939 painting by Harry A. DeYoung. It's doubtful that anyone would stand so casually near an open gate to greet a rider when enemy fire would be pouring in.

CHAPTER FIVE ❧

"Take Care of My Little Boy"

Thursday, March 3, dawned clear and calm, and the temperature rose above forty degrees. Spirits inside the Alamo were high. The arrival of the Gonzales volunteers had brought troop strength to 189 men. These reinforcements had also bolstered the notion that more help might arrive at any moment.

It was possible, those inside the Alamo reasoned, that Travis had been right when he'd said, "The Lord is on our side." They had withstood ten days of bombardment and enemy assaults and not one person—man, woman, or child—had been seriously injured. That suggested that God was watching over them and that, as David defeated Goliath, they might indeed hold off the Mexican troops surrounding them.

> NO ONE IN THE ALAMO EVER TOOK A PRECISE HEAD COUNT OR MADE A COMPLETE LIST OF NAMES. CURRENTLY HISTORIANS HOLD THAT 189 MEN WERE THERE ON THE DAY THE MEXICAN ARMY FINALLY ATTACKED. HISTORIAN THOMAS LINDLEY ASSERTS THAT THE ACTUAL NUMBER SHOULD BE 257, THOUGH HE HAS YET TO FULLY DOCUMENT HIS CLAIM. THE MAYOR OF BÉXAR AT THE TIME, FRANCISCO RUIZ, PUT THE NUMBER AT 182, WHILE TWO MEXICAN OFFICERS SAID THEY COUNTED BETWEEN 250 AND 257.
>
>

A portrait of James Butler Bonham by Charles B. Normann. Because no known contemporary pictures of Bonham exist, this likeness is probably based on his nephew, who was said to greatly resemble Bonham and who had the same first name.

All their hopes came crashing down at eleven o'clock that morning. That was when an exhausted, mud-spattered courier rode his horse past startled Mexican sentries and hurtled safely into the Alamo. The courier was James Bonham, and he had risked his life to report back to Travis. The news he brought was grim.

First, the commander of the Mexican Army's right flank, General Urrea, had been defeating one group of Texan soldiers after another in his march up the coast. A few of the men survived, but most had been put to the sword. More important, Colonel Fannin would not be coming to Travis's aid.

Fannin had tried, Bonham explained. He had led a force of more than three hundred men out of Fort Defiance on the twenty-sixth, along with four cannon and several wagons filled with supplies and ammunition. The relief column managed to travel only two hundred yards before one of the wagons broke down. Two more wagons broke before the men covered the next mile, and while they struggled unsuccessfully to move a stuck ammunition wagon by hand, several of the oxen wandered off. At this point, Fannin decided to pull his men back to the safety of his fort.

Travis gallantly attempted to shrug off Fannin's failure. In a letter to his friend Jesse Grimes written just after he received Bonham's report, Travis wrote: "I am still here, in fine spirits and well to do." But he knew their situation was nearly hopeless, especially when an additional thousand Mexican soldiers entered Béxar late in the afternoon. In that same letter, Travis admitted that the noose was indeed very tight: "They are now encamped under entrenchments, on all sides of us."

The others inside the Alamo knew the truth as well. They had heard the rousing cheers and the sound of the military band as the additional units of Santa Anna's army marched through town. They could see Mexican cannon and soldiers and trenches all around them, and they knew more were moving into position every day.

> *"We . . . hereby resolve and declare, that our political connection with the Mexican nation has forever ended, and that the people of Texas do now constitute a FREE, SOVEREIGN, and INDEPENDENT REPUBLIC and are fully invested with all the rights and attributes which properly belong to independent nations."*
>
> TEXAS DECLARATION OF INDEPENDENCE, MARCH 2, 1836. THE ALAMO DEFENDERS NEVER LEARNED ABOUT THE VOTE TO CREATE AN INDEPENDENT TEXAS.

EVEN THOUGH THEIR CANNON WEREN'T FIRED VERY OFTEN, THE TEXANS ONCE MANAGED TO ACCIDENTALLY HIT SANTA ANNA'S HEADQUARTERS IN TOWN. UNFORTUNATELY FOR THE ALAMO DEFENDERS, THE COMMANDER-IN-CHIEF WAS OUT SCOUTING NEW CANNON PLACEMENT.

Many of Juan Seguín's group decided—just as Philip Dimitt, Benjamin Nobles, and Nat Lewis had earlier—that fighting would be useless. Approximately fifteen of Seguín's men quietly slipped out of the fort and eluded the Mexicans waiting for them. Even the stalwart David Crockett found himself fidgety and nervous. In a rare admission of dissatisfaction, he confided to Susannah Dickinson: "I think we had better march out and die in the open air. I don't like to be hemmed up."

Near midnight, another courier left the Alamo and carefully worked his way through the Mexican lines. In his pocket he carried Travis's dispatches, including a brief, touching note to his friend David Ayers. "Take care of my little boy," he asked Ayers. "If the country should be

⟳ JUAN SEGUÍN ⟲

One of the most loyal backers of the Texas Revolution was twenty-nine-year-old Juan Seguín, a native of Béxar and a captain in the Texan Army's cavalry division.

Seguín was a Tejano who spoke Spanish and English. He came from an important and powerful Béxar family, which meant local citizens respected him and would follow his orders. In short, he was the ideal man to negotiate with Santa Anna during the siege. But there was also an urgent appeal going out to Sam Houston, and Seguín's knowledge of the countryside made him the perfect person to carry the message through enemy lines.

He left the Alamo on February 25, delivered the message, and then began rounding up troops to take back to Béxar. Meanwhile, without his leadership, his company of Tejano horsemen were becoming disillusioned by the way events were unfolding at the Alamo. They faced certain slaughter, and they did not see much point in dying that way. So most of Seguín's men left the Alamo.

Travis—always ready to believe the worst about Mexicans—immediately condemned these Tejanos as deserters, calling them "public enemies." The label would later be applied to all Tejanos, even those who sided with their Texian neighbors in the fight. Many Anglos would simply forget the heroic deeds performed by Seguín and his followers during the rebellion, which included making vital scouting reports before and after the siege of the Alamo.

Following the revolution, Tejanos found themselves the targets of widespread prejudice, repressive laws, and land seizures. The 1840 *Emigrant's Guide to the New Republic* described Tejanos as "far inferior to Anglo-Americans . . . mostly illiterate . . . cowardly and incompetent."

Juan Seguín came under particularly savage attack. He was falsely accused of treason, and his life was threatened. Seguín would eventually lose everything he owned and be forced to flee to Mexico, where he was imprisoned. He returned to Texas years later to restore his good name, but he would forever feel like "a foreigner in my native land."

An 1838 portrait of Captain Juan Seguín by Jefferson Wright. Seguín was a great champion of Texas independence, and he and his men fought hard and provided valuable scouting information that eventually led to Santa Anna's defeat.

saved, I may make him a splendid fortune; but if the country should be lost and I should perish, he will have nothing but the proud recollection that he is the son of a man who died for his country."

The next day, the fourth, was sunny, though a steady wind kept the temperature in the low forties. The Mexicans began a bombardment of the fort early in the morning, but the Alamo guns were silent except for two rounds fired in the afternoon. While there is no record of what went on inside the Alamo that day, it is likely that a deepening gloom took hold. Powder was in short supply, there would be no reinforcements, and the Mexican trenches were being moved closer and closer.

March 5 was a warm, clear day, and Mexican artillery made it even warmer. All through the morning and into the evening the two-cannon battery to the north slammed away at the garrison. The north wall was particularly vulnerable, and it was clear the Mexicans knew this and were trying to weaken it even more.

Once again, the lack of powder meant the Alamo responded with only a few cannon shots throughout the entire day. At around ten o'clock at night, the Mexican barrage tapered off and all firing ceased.

The Alamo defenders sighed with relief and began emerging from cover to stretch their weary legs and cook supper. It had been another miraculous day, they told each other; no one had been killed, and there were no serious injuries. Susannah Dickinson later remembered sharing hot tea with her husband, Almeron, and a very grimy James Bonham. Nearby, the Esparza boys played, while Concepción Losoya prepared a meal for her sons, Juan and Toribio (Toribio was an Alamo defender). These quiet domestic scenes were interrupted when Travis summoned the men into the main plaza.

A photograph of Susannah Dickinson taken approximately twenty years after the fall of the Alamo. She entered the Alamo with her husband, Almeron, and their fifteen-month-old daughter, Angelina. While being led from the chapel by a Mexican officer during the final battle, she received a bullet wound in her right calf; later she provided recollections of what went on during the siege.

Travis did not mince words. They were completely surrounded, he told the men, and it was clear that no help was coming. They now had three choices: they could surrender, they could attempt an escape, or they could fight to the finish. They couldn't hope to win, he pointed out, but they might delay the enemy's advance into Texas. He closed by saying he intended to stay.

"If we succeed the Country is ours. It is immense in extent, and fertile in its soil and will amply reward all our toil. If we fail, then death in the cause of liberty and humanity is not a cause for shuddering. . . . We know what awaits us, and are prepared to meet it."

DANIEL CLOUD IN A LETTER TO HIS FAMILY, DECEMBER 1835

Travis then urged everyone to fight alongside him, though he left the decision up to each man. Madame Candelaria gave several accounts of this meeting, each more dramatic than the one before. In one of her more vivid recollections she had Travis exhorting the men in stirring language: "Let us resolve to withstand our adversaries to the last and at each advance to kill as many of them as possible. And when at last they storm our fortress let us kill them as they come; kill them as they scale our wall; kill them as they leap within; kill them as they raise their weapons and as they use them; kill them as they kill our companions; and continue to kill as long as one of us shall remain alive."

Legend has it that Travis took his sword and drew a line in the dirt in front of him, telling the men that if they intended to fight, they should step across it and join him.

Whatever Travis said and did, it was effective. Every man present chose to stay and fight to the end—every man, that is, but one.

❧ A LINE IN THE DIRT ❧

On March 5, Travis told his men that their situation was hopeless but that he intended to stay and fight the Mexican Army. Legend has it that he then drew a line in the dirt with his sword, telling the men to step over it if they wanted to join him. The entire garrison, except for Louis Rose, did so.

It is a dramatic and inspiring story, and it is also the sort of romantic gesture that Travis would have loved. But did he actually draw a line?

The line was first mentioned in 1873, when William Zuber (who said he had heard it from his parents, who had heard it from Rose) related the tale to a newspaper reporter. After its publication, two Alamo survivors, Enrique Esparza and Susannah Dickinson, took up the story as well.

Yet there are inconsistencies between the Esparza and Dickinson accounts. For instance, at one point Susannah said the line was drawn but that Travis told anyone who wanted to leave to cross it. Later, in 1876, she made a formal statement to the Texas adjutant general that said Travis asked those who wanted to escape "to step out of the ranks" and made no mention of a line in the dirt.

A year later, Zuber also made a statement to the adjutant general in which he confessed to having invented part of Rose's account. He didn't specify which part he had made up, but since a number of newspaper editorials had criticized him severely over the "line in the dirt" reference, it is believed that that is what he was referring to.

Finally, James Allen, the last courier to leave the Alamo, never mentioned the line during his lifetime.

The inconsistencies suggest that Travis did not draw a line in the dirt on March 5. Still, some historians see no harm in a legend that perpetuates the memory of bravery, and they follow the advice offered by J. K. Beretta in the *Southwestern Historical Quarterly:* "Is there any proof that Travis didn't draw the line? If not, then let us believe it."

A fanciful painting by Louis Eyth showing Travis speaking to the Alamo defenders after drawing the legendary line in the dirt.

Angelina Dickinson was one of the youngest survivors of the Alamo siege; she became known as "the babe of the Alamo."

The only man who chose to leave was Louis Rose. He was fifty years old and had seen battle in Napoleon's Grand Army; for him, the important thing about any battle was living to fight another day. From his sickbed, his old friend Jim Bowie tried to persuade him to stay, but Rose would have none of it.

Late that night, under cover of dark, he slid over a wall and edged his way downriver until he came to a ford. He waded across, dodged along a street, and escaped into open country several minutes later. No one challenged him in town, and Rose remembered later that this had seemed odd to him.

Louis Rose was able to escape so easily because at midnight Santa Anna had begun moving his troops in preparation for the early-morning attack. As always, the commander-in-chief himself dictated the battle orders, which were remarkable for their focus on the smallest of details. Santa Anna instructed the officers on the amount of ammunition each soldier should be given, what the men should wear, and the number of scaling ladders, crowbars, and axes each advancing column should bring, as well as how to carry them. He even admonished the men to wear the chin straps of their tall black shakos (military hats) correctly. "These," he warned, "the commander will watch closely."

Tiny details aside, the battle orders called for the Alamo to be attacked at four different points at the same time. This would ensure that the Alamo defenders would be spread out along the walls and would not be able to concentrate their firepower at any one spot. And while many historians insist that the Mexican soldiers involved were inexperienced and inept, Santa Anna expressly ordered that "the untrained recruits . . . remain in the camps."

There were no specific directions concerning prisoners, though one sentence suggested how they should be dealt with. "All armaments will be in good shape," the commander-in-chief reminded his men, "especially the bayonets."

A thick cover of clouds after dark hid the moon and the movements of the Mexican soldiers. They were warned by commanding officers not to smoke or talk and to walk slowly and carefully. Everything depends on a surprise attack, they were told. Your life depends on it.

To be certain that every man went into battle in the proper fighting spirit, they were read the final lines of Santa Anna's battle orders: "Take this into consideration: Against the daring foreigners opposing us, the Honor of our Nation and Army is at stake. [I expect] each man to fulfill his duties and to exert himself to give his country a day of glory and satisfaction."

"The time has come to strike a decisive blow upon the enemy occupying the fortress of the Alamo."
GENERAL SANTA ANNA TO HIS TROOPS

Patriotism and honor were all well and good, but Santa Anna knew that many of his soldiers needed a more tangible incentive. Bring me victory, he told them in the closing line, and remember that I know "how to reward those brave men who form The Army of Operations."

Eighteen hundred Mexican soldiers moved through the night, circling wide around the Alamo. Fourteen hundred were in the attack columns; four hundred were held in reserve. Their movements went completely undetected despite the fact that Travis had stationed three men outside the walls with express orders to listen for the enemy. In all likelihood, these sentries and just about everyone else

❧ JOSÉ DE LA PEÑA ❧

José Enrique de la Peña was eighteen when he joined the Mexican Navy in 1825. It's very likely that he began writing soon after this, because we know he had several articles published three years later under the pseudonym Lover of the Navy.

He transferred out of the navy in 1828, and after Santa Anna became president in 1833, de la Peña was made a captain of cavalry. By the time the Texas Revolution began, he had been reduced to the rank of lieutenant, though it is not known why he had been demoted.

During the Alamo siege, he was assigned to the battalion that was to make the assault on the north wall. He made several trips to and from the rear lines with messages while the battle raged, and it seems that he sustained a head injury. He later received letters from a number of senior officers citing his bravery and was eventually restored to the rank of captain.

In 1837, de la Peña took part in a failed uprising against Santa Anna in support of the Constitution of 1824, for which he was jailed.

Two years later, while still in prison, he wrote an article about the Alamo siege. His memoirs came to light in the mid-1970s when John Peace, a lawyer and the chairman of the University of Texas Board of Regents, bought them and other de la Peña papers from the widow of a Mexican antiques dealer.

The memoirs contain a great deal of information about Santa Anna's campaign to retake Texas, including the fight at the Alamo. They also claim that one of those who survived the battle was David Crockett. Many historians believe that de la Peña's memoirs are one of the best sources of detailed information we have about the Alamo; others attack them as inaccurate or even completely fraudulent.

In 1998, the de la Peña memoirs and other papers were sold at auction to two unidentified Texans for approximately three hundred fifty thousand dollars. Scholars hope that the new owners will allow them to study the original documents and test them carefully for authenticity. So far, this has not been the case.

inside the fort, exhausted by days of bombardment, simply fell asleep at their posts.

Sometime in the dead of the night one of the Alamo gates was slowly opened, followed a second later by the frantic pounding of hooves. The last Alamo courier, sixteen-year-old James Allen, raced off, crossed the Mexican lines, and darted up the road to Goliad with another—and final—desperate plea for help.

"If we fail here get to the river with the children all Texas will be before the enemy. . . . There is no discontent in our boys some are tired from loss of sleep and rest. . . . I don't know what else to say they is calling for all letters, kiss the dear children for me be well & God protects us all. . . .
I hope you get this & know—I love you all."

ISAAC MILLSAPS IN A LETTER TO HIS WIFE, MARCH 3, 1836

By five o'clock in the morning, all the Mexican troops were in position exactly where Santa Anna had ordered them to be, one musket shot's distance from the Alamo. The quiet—the first unbroken spell of it in almost twelve days—was unearthly. Lieutenant de la Peña was one of the officers about to charge the fort, and he recalled that "this half-light, the silence we kept . . . the coolness of the morning air, the great quietude that seemed to prolong the hours, and the dangers we would soon have to face, all of this rendered our situation grave."

His fellow soldiers were "still breathing and able to communicate," de la Peña noted. But he understood something else as well. In just a few minutes, many of the men beside him would be dead, and "returned to the nothingness whence we had come."

Jean Louis Theodore Gentilz's 1885 painting of the fall of the Alamo. While there are numerous inaccuracies in this picture (it is much too bright, for one thing), the buildings are based on sketches Gentilz made before renovations were done.

CHAPTER SIX

"It Was But a Small Affair"

Atiny bit of light appeared on the horizon, a pale, ghostly illumination far to the east. It was then that José María Gonzalez received the signal from Santa Anna, put his bugle to his lips, and played the field command "at attention." Instantly, fourteen hundred Mexican soldiers pushed themselves up from the damp grass and surged forward.

The attack was such a surprise that the three sleeping sentries were never able to raise an alarm or fire a shot. They were overcome by the running attackers and quickly dispatched, the first Alamo defenders to die.

As the Mexicans neared the fort, Santa Anna ordered a change in music and had the military band play the *degüello*. This was a medieval song that had originated during Spain's long and bloody war with the Moors. Its name translated as "to slit the throat" or "to behead," and its bloodcurdling strains were meant to inspire courage in the charging troops.

Captain John Baugh was on the Alamo walls beginning rounds when he heard the initial Mexican bugle. Startled, he glanced out into the blackness, not knowing exactly what was happening. Then he heard a sustained, mass shouting coming closer and closer: *"Viva Santa Anna! Viva Santa Anna! Viva Santa Anna!"*

Baugh turned and bellowed for everyone inside the Alamo to hear: "The Mexicans are coming!"

The music for the degüello, *the ancient call to fight to the death with no mercy, which accompanied Mexican soldiers as they charged the Alamo.*

Travis bolted awake in an instant and sprinted toward the northeast artillery battery, trailed by his slave, Joe, both of them armed with shotguns. Along the way, the young commander shouted, "Come on, boys. The Mexicans are upon us, and we'll give them hell." When he encountered the few remaining members of Juan Seguín's company, he switched briefly to Spanish. *"No rendirse, muchachos."* ("No surrender, my friends.")

The columns of Mexican soldiers were hard to spot in the dark landscape, but their continued shouting betrayed their whereabouts. "The officers were unable to repress this act of folly," Lieutenant de la Peña lamented, "which was paid for dearly."

Texans were now awake and at their positions, firing toward the sound of the voices as rapidly as possible. Their cannon awoke too, booming one, and another, and another round into the advancing troops. The very first shot from the cannon nearest Travis sent nearly fifty Mexicans, including one of their captains, to that "nothingness" de la Peña had mentioned. It also seriously wounded their commander and three other high-ranking officers. The column under General Cós suffered forty men killed in the opening volley.

"There is no doubt that some would have regretted not being among the first to meet the enemy, for it was considered an honor to be counted among the first."

LIEUTENANT JOSÉ DE LA PEÑA IN HIS MEMOIRS

A rain of musket balls, shotgun pellets, grapeshot, chopped-up horseshoes, and pieces of scrap iron fell on the heads of the advancing Mexicans. The shouting turned to screams as the wounded dropped in batches, shoulders ripped open, leg bones snapped, faces mutilated. Battalion commander Colonel Francisco Duque went down with a shattered leg and was trampled by his men in the confusion.

The front lines wavered but were urged on by the officers and the press of the men behind. On they stumbled, driven by duty and fear and anger, over the unfamiliar terrain and their dead comrades, across the irrigation ditch, always moving toward the fort that now pulsed like some living creature in the flash and flame of rifles and cannon.

The Mexican cannon were silent during the assault, fearing they would hit their own soldiers. Those charging did fire off their muskets, though stopping to aim properly was out of the question. They fired clumsily from the hip while on the run. Even so, a swarm of .75-caliber balls whistled past the heads of the Alamo defenders, chipped away at the walls near them, and occasionally found flesh.

The final battle has begun.

There was no stopping to help wounded friends, no time to think or worry or lament. Each Texan poured in powder, rammed in a ball, aimed as well as possible, and pulled the trigger.

And still the Mexican soldiers came on, despite the withering fire and their staggering losses. A few even managed to reach the wall under Travis and began to put up a scaling ladder.

Travis understood the threat immediately. But this close to the wall, fire from artillery could not touch the enemy below. So he and Joe leaned out over the wall, aimed their shotguns, and discharged them at point-blank range into the upraised faces of the enemy.

Travis never knew the effect of his blast. Just as he squeezed the trigger, a volley of Mexican rifles erupted from the dark and a single ball found its mark, striking Travis in the forehead. His shotgun dropped from his hands as he spun and then toppled down the dirt embankment behind him.

He managed to sit up in the dirt, but he was so badly injured he was unable to do more. Joe was at his side seconds later but could do nothing for his fatally wounded master. As Travis drifted into unconsciousness, Joe fled to the long barracks and hid in a windowless room, listening and waiting.

Travis's and Joe's shotgun fire, along with the fire of others on the wall, produced immediate results. The Mexican soldiers huddled there began a hasty retreat, and the forward momentum of the two columns from the north was halted. But these weren't amateur soldiers ready to break and run at the first opposition; they were veterans. As soon as they heard the commands of their officers, they turned and pushed forward a second time.

Once again, they swarmed toward the walls of the Alamo; once again, a hail of metal chopped scores of them down and forced them to retreat, this time in chaos.

While all this was happening on the north side of the fort, the columns to the east and south had run into their own problems. Both had advanced bravely only to be subjected to deadly rifle fire and a horrific cannon barrage. The two lines of men were easy targets for Texans on top of the low barracks and chapel, in the lunette, and behind the dirt-and-wood palisade. Instead of marching doggedly to certain death, these men instinctively sought cover and remained pinned down for five minutes or more.

From his vantage point with the northern battery, Santa Anna viewed the scene with growing alarm. Instead of soldiers scaling ladders against the fortress wall, he saw a snarled mass of confused men

The enemies meet at the wall. Lajos Markos's painting contains several contradictions: for example, Travis, pictured in the center, was dead before the enemy climbed the walls. Even so, the artist does depict fighters on both sides as determined and extremely brave.

and possible defeat. Extremely agitated, the commander-in-chief ordered the four hundred reserves to join the fight for the north wall. Then he ordered every one of his startled staff officers into the fray, with instructions to encourage the men.

"This gallant reserve merely added to the noise and the victims," de la Peña lamented. "Before [this] battalion, advancing through a shower of bullets and volley of shrapnel, had a chance to reach the foot of the walls, half their officers were wounded."

The reserves managed to fire off their rifles while on the run, which proved disastrous for the troops in front of them. General Filisola thought that as many as one-quarter of all Mexican casualties were caused by this "friendly fire."

The Mexican troops were being mauled and were on the verge of retreating. "A quarter of an hour had elapsed," de la Peña recalled, "during which our soldiers remained in a terrible situation. . . ."

Then, in a flash, everything changed. The column to the east near the corral began moving again, though not directly toward the fort. Instead, it turned north and soon joined up with the column at the northeast corner. "All united at one point," recalled de la Peña, "mixing and forming a confused mass." Around the same time, General Cós's men went to the left and attacked the northern portion of the west wall, where an opening had been barricaded with wood and dirt.

"One can but admire the stubborn resistance of our enemy, and the constant bravery of all our troops. It seemed every cannon ball or pistol shot of the enemy embedded itself in the breasts of our men who without stopping cried: 'Long live the Mexican republic! Long live General Santa Anna!' "
ANONYMOUS MEXICAN SOLDIER IN A LETTER HOME

Ruth Conerly painted this heroic but almost wholly inaccurate scene of Travis battling the enemy. Travis was dead long before the Mexicans were able to scale the north wall.

All these soldiers—well over a thousand of them—were easy targets for the Alamo defenders, who had rushed from various positions around the fort to help their comrades on the north wall. Battered and bloodied, the Mexican soldiers next to the wall began to climb it, some using ladders, most clawing their way up the rough timbers used to patch the gaping hole there.

At this moment the fourth column to the south chose to strike again. Wisely, they skirted the palisades, where David Crockett and his Tennessee Boys blazed away with deadly accuracy. They sprinted to the southeast corner of the Alamo, where the eighteen-pounder held command.

This time, probably because so many Texans were busy defending the north wall, these soldiers met little resistance. They soon climbed the wall, bayoneted the gunners, and seized the big cannon. Next, they poured down the earthen ramp into the main plaza, some going toward the main gate, low barracks, and chapel, others hurrying toward the north wall and the backs of the Texans.

A second later a handful of Mexican soldiers pulled themselves up and over the north wall. One of the first to drop inside the Alamo was fifty-five-year-old General Juan V. Amador. Two days before, he had been relieved of all duty by Santa Anna for some minor incident. Leading his men over the wall erased his disgrace; surviving was nothing short of a miracle.

As fighting on the north wall intensified, Cós's men pushed through the opening in the west wall and rushed forward.

De la Peña was at the north wall, and his account of the minutes that followed captures the confusion and mayhem. "The first to climb were thrown down by bayonets already waiting for them behind the parapet, or by pistol fire, but the courage of our soldiers was not diminished as they saw their comrades falling dead or wounded, and they hurried to occupy their places and to avenge them, climbing over their bleeding bodies. The sharp reports of the rifles, the whistling of bullets, the groans of the wounded, the cursing of the men, the sighs and anguished cries of the dying, the arrogant harangues of the officers, the noise of the instruments of war, and the inordinate shouts of the attackers, who climbed vigorously, bewildered all and made of this moment a tremendous and critical one. The shouting of those being attacked was no less loud and from the beginning had pierced our ears with desperate, terrible cries of alarm in a language we did not understand."

Vicious hand-to-hand combat followed, with rifle butts, bayonets, knives, axes, ramrods, and anything else handy. Despite a valiant effort by the Alamo's defenders, the fight for the north wall was over quickly. There were simply too many Mexicans coming from too many sides for the Texans to defend themselves. Everywhere they turned, an enemy rushed at them with bayonet extended.

While he is often referred to as Santa Anna's inept brother-in-law, General Cós led his men ably in their assault on the west wall.

A highly imaginative idea of what went on inside the Alamo compound during the battle. For one thing, Santa Anna (on horse in center) was nowhere near the actual fighting. For another, the gable hump on the chapel was not added until the 1840s.

Most of the women and children were huddled inside the chapel when the walls of the fort were breached and the fighting moved into the main plaza. "We could hear the Mexican officers shouting to the men to jump over [the walls]," said Enrique Esparza. "Men were fighting so close that we could hear them strike each other."

Almeron Dickinson found his wife in the dim interior and blurted out, "Good God, Sue, the Mexicans are inside our walls! All is lost! If they spare you, save my child!" He then kissed her, drew his sword, and bounded out of the room to rejoin his men on the chapel roof. Susannah never saw her husband again.

A few minutes later her sixteen-year-old friend from Gonzales, Galba Fuqua, stumbled in. "I looked at him in horror," Susannah later recalled. "He was holding his jaws together with his hands. Blood trickled from his mouth. He tried to speak to me, then with an agonizing gaze tried to make me understand." Was he trying to communicate some last words for his family and friends? Susannah never knew, because "the boy turned and ran out to his death."

Outside in the main plaza, the battle had entered a different phase. When it was clear that they could no longer keep the Mexicans out, John Baugh signaled for the Alamo defenders to withdraw, according to a prearranged plan, to rooms lining the main plaza.

A number of the men panicked, however. Eliel Melton and anywhere from sixty to sixty-seven others jumped the palisade walls and tried to race to safety. Santa Anna—a man who didn't let many details escape his attention—had foreseen such an action. The Texans hadn't gone far when Mexican cavalry swept down, slashing them with sabers and piercing them with lances.

Several escaped immediate death. One man burrowed under a bush, while another hid beneath the bridge spanning the San Antonio River. Both were later discovered and killed.

Two unidentified men showed up in Nacogdoches at the end of March and claimed to have survived the "massacre" at Béxar. Their

Artist Henry Arthur McArdle has played fast and loose with perspective and historical fact, but his massive seven-by-twelve-foot canvas certainly captures the chaos and confusion of hand-to-hand combat.

story has some credibility because it appeared in a local newspaper one week before the fall of the Alamo was officially announced.

And one young man, jockey Henry Warnell, is generally accepted as being a survivor of the Alamo. He was a small man who weighed less than 118 pounds, but he was surprisingly strong, and clever. Warnell struggled across the prairie and ended up either at Dimmit's Landing or at Linville. He died three months later of wounds he had received during the battle or his escape.

These men aside, most Alamo defenders stayed and met their fate within the fort. They surrendered the walls and cannon placements and backed down the dirt ramps or jumped from the roofs into the main plaza. There they fought their way inch by inch to the rooms lining the inside of the fort. As they did, waves of Mexican soldiers came over the walls and streamed into the fort.

Travis had prepared for this moment: he had ordered small holes punched through the walls of some rooms. As hundreds upon hundreds of Mexicans swarmed into the main plaza and charged the living quarters, gunfire spit at them from those loopholes.

Seeing their fellow soldiers being slaughtered below them, Mexican officers ordered the Alamo cannon turned inward and began blasting away at doors. Too many soldiers "nearing the doors and blind with fury and smoke," de la Peña noted, "fired their shots against friends and enemies alike, and in this way our losses were most grievous."

Doors were blown apart or kicked open, rooms were entered, and men from both sides were shot, stabbed, or clubbed to death. A killing frenzy had seized everyone involved, and not even the officers could contain it.

General Cós had a bugler blow the cease-fire, but nobody paid attention. "A horrible carnage took place," de la Peña commented. "The tumult was great, the disorder frightful; it seemed as if the furies had descended upon us. . . ."

The doors of the low barracks crashed open, and in rushed Mexican soldiers. In one of the rooms they discovered Jim Bowie and killed him. Another door in the low barracks swung open, and Gertrudis Navarro appeared, begging the soldiers not to shoot into the room. "When Señorita Gertrudis opened the door," recalled Juana Alsbury, "she was greeted in offensive language by the soldiers. Her shawl was torn from her shoulders, and she rushed back into the room."

A soldier asked where Gertrudis's husband was and then demanded her money. At that moment, Alamo defender Edwin Mitchell rushed to aid the women but was quickly bayoneted. No sooner did Mitchell's body hit the floor than a follower of Juan Seguín entered the room, chased by other soldiers. He was immediately stabbed four or five times, then shot repeatedly.

The Mexican soldiers then set to ransacking the room. They soon broke open Juana's trunk, in which the officers of the Alamo had stored their valuables. An extremely agitated Mexican officer entered the room soon after, wanting to know why women and children were in the fort. He then had the two women and the baby stand near a cannon in the plaza that was being loaded to demolish barracks doors. Another Mexican officer spotted them in this dangerous position and told them to get away. Suddenly, out of the smoke emerged a relative of

❧ THE DEATH OF JIM BOWIE ❧

We know Jim Bowie was seriously ill during the siege of the Alamo. We also know he was confined to a room in the low barracks during the final fight. But how did he die?

Several stories have been offered. One has Bowie propped up in bed, pistols blazing away, as Mexican soldiers crashed through the door to his room. This is the one favored in the movies, and it usually has several dead Mexican soldiers crumpled around his bed.

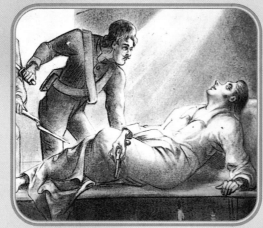

Another story says that Bowie was too sick to defend himself and might even have been unconscious when he was stabbed or shot repeatedly.

A third has Bowie either dead or committing suicide by blowing his own brains out before the Mexicans got to him.

And a fourth was offered by Captain José Juan Sánchez Navarro: "The perverse and braggart Santiago Bowie died like a woman, hidden almost under the mattress."

Which is true? As with many conflicting details about the siege and attack of the Alamo, there is no definite answer.

A detail from Louis Eyth's painting of the death of Jim Bowie.

It seems unlikely that Bowie either killed himself or hid from the Mexicans. Bowie never ran from a fight, even when the odds were against him. He certainly didn't cower inside the Alamo when the Mexican Army first appeared on February 23; he risked his life to ensure the safety of his sisters-in-law and one of their children, then galloped out again to round up food for the garrison. What is more, if he had had the strength to hold a weapon, his nature would have made him get up to face the enemy with his comrades. He would not have lingered in bed waiting to be killed.

We are left then with his being already dead, unconscious, or extremely feeble when the Mexicans found him. None of these choices seems to befit a man whose whole life was one of action and courage, so most historians choose to close out Jim Bowie's life with a quote from his mother. "So Jim is dead?" she is supposed to have said on hearing the news. "I'll wager they found no wounds in his back."

Juana's from Béxar, Manuel Perez, who had come to watch the battle, accompanied by an unidentified female slave of Jim Bowie. Perez put Juana, Gertrudis, and the baby in the care of this woman and took them to the chapel, where they joined the other women and children already there.

Meanwhile, inside both barracks, a horrific room-by-room battle was raging. While several Mexican accounts state that one or more of the Texans showed the white flag of surrender, most did their best to take the lives of as many Mexican soldiers as possible. Once again, however, there were simply too many of the enemy pouring in through the doors. The rebels kept up an hour of vicious fighting, but finally Mexicans entered the last of the rooms and put those inside to the sword.

Outside in the main plaza a young Mexican officer, Lieutenant José María Torres, glanced up from the fighting and was immediately incensed. There atop the long barracks was an azure banner trimmed with gold fringe. It was probably the flag of the First Company of the New Orleans Greys, but the impetuous Torres saw it as a symbol of rebellion and decided to do something about it.

He raced to the offending flag only to discover that other Mexican soldiers had been there before him. At the base of the flagpole lay the bodies of three sergeants, shot dead before they could pull the flag down.

Torres was undaunted. He was about to rip the offending symbol from the pole when Lieutenant Damasio Martínez arrived to help. Seconds later, Martínez was shot dead, most likely by Texans on the chapel roof. Torres did not hesitate. He tore the banner off and raised the red, white, and green flag of Mexico. Such acts are what legends are made of, and Torres's heroic act was witnessed by many of his friends.

Torres secured his country's flag and stepped back—and was rewarded with a one-ounce lead ball that dropped him, mortally wounded.

The battle then entered its final moments. The only position still held by the Texans and still issuing fire was the chapel. Enrique Esparza had vivid recollections of these last moments many decades later. "The end came suddenly," he recalled in 1907. He was huddled with his mother, two brothers, and sister in the main room of the chapel. Above on the roof his father, Gregorio, was already dead, while other Alamo defenders hid in dark corners of the building.

"Suddenly," Enrique recalled, "there was a terrible din. Cannon boomed. Their shot crashed through the doors and windows and the breaches in the walls. Then men rushed in on us. They swarmed among us and over us. They fired on us in vollies. They struck us down with their (muskets). In the dark our men groped and grasped

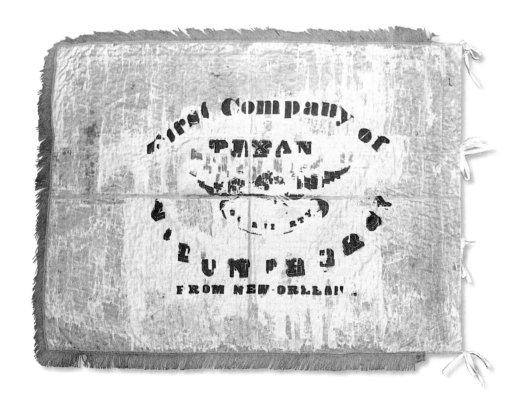

The flag of the New Orleans Greys as photographed in Mexico City in 1980. Many flags are believed to have been flown at the Alamo, but this is one of only two known for certain to have been waving during the final assault.

Mexican soldiers close in on a small band of Alamo defenders.

the throats of our foe-men and buried their knives into their hearts."

Mexican officers would later apologize for the savage behavior of their troops. After weeks of brutal marching that had taken the lives of comrades, wives, and children, after thirteen days of tense siege warfare and a terror-filled charge, they went berserk. They stabbed and shot anything they considered an enemy, alive or dead, old or young. Even the barracks cat was cornered and executed, the soldiers shouting, "It is not a cat, but an American." At least one woman, possibly Bowie's slave, was hacked to death, as well as one child.

"By my side was an American boy," Enrique said, referring to one of Anthony Wolfe's sons. "He was about my age but larger. As they reached us he rose to his feet. . . . He was unarmed. They slew him where he stood and his corpse fell over me."

Up on the roof, near the artillery, Anthony Wolfe grabbed his other son in his arms and jumped over the side. Whether he was trying to commit suicide or escape is not known; both died as a result of the fall.

Several defenders remained alive in the chapel, and these fled to the room where Susannah Dickinson was. Three were quickly gunned down, and one, Jacob Walker, was hoisted on bayonets "like a bundle of fodder," according to Susannah.

Major Robert Evans came into the chapel next, severely wounded and crawling painfully toward the rear, where the last remaining barrels of powder were stored. As chief ordnance officer, he might have been there to get more powder. It's also possible he was attempting to carry out a final, desperate order of Travis's—to blow up the Alamo and as many of the enemy as possible. Whatever his mission was, he managed to grab a burning torch, but before he could reach the powder, he was shot and killed.

Of the 189 men who had defied Santa Anna's army, only a small number survived the initial slaughter. One man, twenty-six-year-old Brigido Guerrero, was about to be killed, but his desperate begging for mercy stayed the bayonets. Guerrero had deserted Santa Anna's army early in the siege and joined the rebels. But now, facing death, he claimed he had been taken prisoner and held against his will. He even said he'd tried to escape to rejoin his comrades but the rebels had been too vigilant. The Mexicans believed his story, and his life was spared.

As many as six others, including a fourteen-year-old boy, surrendered to General Manuel Fernandez Castrillón. Castrillón was a man of honor, and he personally guaranteed the men's safety as prisoners. Several minutes later, Santa Anna learned about the survivors and ordered the men executed despite his general's promise. "I do not want to see these men living," Santa Anna is supposed to have said. Several of his officers then stepped forward and, according to de la Peña, hacked the men to death with their swords.

This incident is recalled today for more than its brutality. Four Mexican officers wrote accounts of the battle stating that one of those who surrendered was none other than David Crockett. Like so many other Alamo reports, their truth can never be proved. When the men inside the Alamo died, a great many of the facts and details that they alone knew or could verify were lost with them.

What is true is that aside from Travis's slave, Joe, the women and children, and two or three defenders, everyone inside the Alamo died on March 6, including David Crockett. By six-thirty in the morning the sounds of battle had ceased and the sun rose, lighting up the fort.

Commander-in-Chief Antonio López de Santa Anna came through the main gate to survey the battle scene. The irrigation ditch, riverbank, cannon placements, barracks rooms, main plaza, and rooftops were littered with the twisted, mangled bodies of the dead. Blood was everywhere. Almost every Alamo defender and between four hundred and six

This painting, called The Last Stand in the Alamo, *shows hand-to-hand combat inside the barracks.*

❧ The Death of David Crockett ❧

One of the most hotly argued debates about the Alamo siege is whether David Crockett died fighting or whether he surrendered and, after pleading for his life, was executed.

Rumors that Crockett had surrendered began circulating within weeks of the fall of the Alamo. The argument that he surrendered is based on the eyewitness accounts of Santa Anna's personal secretary, Ramón Caro, and several Mexican officers, including Lieutenant de la Peña, Captain Navarro, Colonel Juan Almonte, and Captain Fernando Urizza.

Those who accept the surrender theory believe that these accounts are essentially correct, even if there are differences in some of the details. Opponents of the theory point out the numerous discrepancies and contradictions among these versions. For example, none of them agree on how many Alamo defenders surrendered and were executed, with their counts ranging from one to seven. There are even conflicts over how the prisoners were killed, some accounts saying by firing squad, others by bayonet and sword.

Both Susannah Dickinson and Travis's slave, Joe, thought Crockett had fallen in action, though neither actually saw him killed. They spotted his body after the battle amid heaps of the dead, both Mexican soldiers and Alamo defenders. Of course, each of their accounts has its own list of inaccuracies and inconsistencies.

So there is testimony for both sides, and none of it is conclusive. Because of this, the only thing we can say for sure is that Crockett died in the Alamo.

A wood engraving shows Crockett being shot by a Mexican soldier.

hundred Mexicans—one-third of the attack force—had been killed, while hundreds of other Mexican soldiers lay wounded and groaning in pain.

"In our opinion all that bloodshed of our soldiers as well as of our enemies was useless, having as its only objective an inconsiderate, childish and culpable vanity so it might be proclaimed that Béxar had been reconquered by force of arms and that in the attack many men had died on both sides."

GENERAL VICENTE FILISOLA IN HIS MEMOIRS

Santa Anna approached Captain Fernando Urizza and glanced around at the carnage of the one-and-a-half-hour battle. "Much blood has been shed," he remarked casually, "but the battle is over; it was but a small affair."

An obviously cruel Santa Anna inspects the Alamo dead after the battle in this painting by Joseph Hefter. Crockett's body lies atop a pile of bodies near the southwest corner of the chapel.

CHAPTER SEVEN

"Remember the Alamo"

After the battle, Santa Anna made a thorough inspection of the Alamo compound, and even had the mayor of Béxar point out the bodies of the famous trio named Bowie, Travis, and Crockett. The women and children were marched through the carnage and taken to a house in Béxar to await their fate. Susannah Dickinson remembered stepping carefully over "heaps of dead and dying" and seeing Crockett's mutilated body "between the church and the two-story barracks building."

Santa Anna then decided to add a final insult to the fallen Alamo defenders. Dead Mexican soldiers, he directed, would be carted to Campo Santo Cementerio to be buried in consecrated ground. The bodies of the rebels would be cremated.

AMONG THE DEAD WAS A YOUNG BLACK MAN NAMED JOHN, WHOSE LAST NAME WAS NEVER RECORDED. JOHN WAS A CLERK IN A BÉXAR STORE OWNED BY FRANCIS L. DESAUQUE AND MAY HAVE BEEN A FREEMAN. JOHN ACCOMPANIED DESAUQUE TO THE ALAMO AND TOOK AN ACTIVE PART IN THE FIGHTING.

At the time, cremation was no longer being practiced by Christians. They believed that the body had to be whole when buried if it was to rise again at Christ's Second Coming. Santa Anna viewed the rebels as heretics and did not want to honor them with a proper burial.

The bodies of the Alamo dead are burned in José Cisneros's Alamo Funeral Pyre.

Soldiers began the difficult task of separating the bodies. The uniforms and skin of many combatants had been burned by exploding gunpowder, and a number of heads had been severed by cannon blasts or swords. All these faces had to be wiped clean before they could be identified.

The bodies of Mexican soldiers were put in oxcarts and hauled off to the cemetery for burial in a mass grave. Many bodies fell or were thrown into the San Antonio River as the carts creaked across the tiny wooden bridge. It's very likely that the bodies of the Alamo defenders who were killed outside the fort were thrown into the river.

Meanwhile, three huge funeral pyres were constructed. The bodies of Alamo defenders were tossed on top of a layer of kindling and wood. More kindling and wood was piled on, and then more bodies. Only one Alamo defender was spared this fate. Earlier in the day, Francisco

Esparza, the brother of Gregorio Esparza, had asked Santa Anna to allow him to bury his brother at Campo Santo. The commander-in-chief graciously said yes, possibly because Francisco had remained loyal to Mexico.

Around five o'clock, as the sun sank low in the west, the pyres were set on fire. Pablo Diaz, a teenager in Béxar, "saw an immense pillar of flame shoot up a short distance [from] the Alamo and the dense smoke from it rise high in the clouds."

"Why is it that Santa Anna always wants to mark his triumphs with blood and tears?"

LIEUTENANT COLONEL JOSÉ JUAN SÁNCHEZ NAVARRO IN HIS DIARY

The fires burned for three days straight, with soldiers throwing on more and more wood. Finally, the flames subsided and curious people emerged from their homes to view the scene. "I saw thousands of vultures flying overhead," Diaz recalled. "As I reached the ford in the river my gaze encountered a terrible sight. The stream was congested with corpses. . . . I halted, horrified, and watched the vultures in their revel and shuddered at the sickening sight."

Diaz hurried past the bloated bodies and the foul stench and made his way to the smoldering ashes of the fire, around which a crowd had gathered. "Fragments of flesh, bone and charred wood and ashes" were everywhere. "Grease that had exuded from the bodies saturated the earth for several feet beyond the ashes and smoldering mesquite branches. The odor was more sickening than that from the corpses in the river. I turned my head aside and left the place in shame."

The remains of the Alamo defenders would lie where they had been burned, exposed to wind, sun, rain, and animals. No officials from the rebel military or government ever came to inspect the scene of battle or attend to the dead. It would be more than a year before Captain Juan Seguín—a faithful friend—could return to gather up what was left of his Alamo friends and fellow revolutionaries and see their remains buried in a nearby peach orchard.

While the funeral pyres were still burning, Santa Anna had the captured women and children brought to him. He interviewed the women one at a time, asking them a series of questions and then releasing them after giving each a blanket and two silver coins. Unknown to the women, this was part of Santa Anna's propaganda strategy aimed at helping him subdue Texas. Colonists would hear about the might of his army and his wrath, but they would also hear about his kindness to these innocent bystanders. Those who had remained loyal to Mexico—mainly Tejano settlers—would be reassured that if they submitted peacefully, they would be treated fairly.

Joe was also given special attention by Santa Anna. Joe was an intelligent and well-spoken man, and Santa Anna wanted to use him as his voice to the colonists. To this end, the general treated Joe to a grand review of his troops, bragging that his army numbered eight thousand men. He then had Joe take a warning to the Texian colonists outside Béxar: Santa Anna and his troops would soon be coming for them.

Having set his propaganda scheme in motion, Santa Anna turned his attention to the military side of his campaign. His army would strike out across Texas in three avenging columns, with a large force trailing behind as reinforcements.

Seven days after the fall of the Alamo, Santa Anna turned his army loose on Texas.

In the weeks to follow, Santa Anna's propaganda machine and his army were amazingly effective. Texian colonists learned about the

massacre at the Alamo and scurried back toward the eastern border. Fear turned to panic when they heard that the hapless Colonel Fannin and just about his entire garrison at Goliad had been captured by the Mexican column led by General Urrea and summarily executed.

Also retreating was the Texan Army, a ragtag group of 374 soldiers commanded by Sam Houston. Houston considered the size of Santa Anna's army and then did the smart thing—he ran. "By falling back," Houston reassured David Burnet, the man elected president of Texas at the recent convention, "Texas can rally and defeat any force that can come against her."

His words did little to calm Burnet or anyone else. The new government and tens of thousands of men, women, and children living in the path of the Mexican Army fled in panic. A scout for the Texan Army, Noah Smithwick, recalled retreating through an abandoned and desolate land: "Houses were standing open, the beds unmade, the breakfast

Sam Houston's son, Andrew Jackson Houston, painted this version of the Goliad soldiers being marched to their slaughter.

⚜ SAM HOUSTON ⚜

Sam Houston was a sight to behold. Standing six feet four inches tall, he had very broad shoulders and piercing gray eyes. He added to the impact by dressing in wildly colorful, eccentric clothes, combinations of Native American, Mexican, Arabian, and European designs. Despite his conspicuously outlandish exterior, he had a rare gift to inspire and lead other men.

As a member of the U.S. Army, he earned rapid promotion for valiant fighting during the War of 1812 and made a lifetime friend of his commanding general, Andrew Jackson. Later he became a lawyer, was elected district attorney of Nashville, became a major general in the militia, served two terms in Congress, and then became governor of Tennessee in 1827 when he was just thirty-four years old.

He went to Texas in 1833 and immediately fell in love with what he saw: a land big enough to fulfill his dreams of wealth and power. After the revolution, Houston would again prove popular with voters. He was twice elected president of the Republic of Texas. When Texas was annexed to the United States, he served from 1846 to 1859 as one of its senators, and after that as its governor.

His life did have a number of rocky spots.

His first marriage ended in a scandal that eventually led to his resignation as governor of Tennessee. He was known to chew opium, and he drank so much that the Cherokees, who genuinely liked him, called him *Oo-tse-tee Ar-dee-tah-skee*—Big Drunk. His failure to respond to Travis's repeated calls for aid also called his conduct into question.

On March 6, before anyone knew of the fall of the Alamo, Houston left Washington-on-the-Brazos for Gonzales, saying he intended to "relieve the brave men in the Alamo." He seems to have moved rather slowly, since it took him five days to cover a distance that shouldn't have taken him more than two.

Along the way, a Texian settler, W. W. Thompson, asked Houston what he thought about the siege of the Alamo, and Houston "swore that he believed it to be a damn lie, & that all those reports from Travis and Fannin were lies, for there are no Mexican forces there and that he believed that it was only electioneering schemes on [the part of] Travis & Fannin to sustain their own popularity."

Years later, Houston would remember his failure and privately confess, "It was a bad business. I hated it."

Sam Houston liked to dress up in costumes. This painting of him as Roman senator at the ruins of Carthage was done in 1831 while he was struggling to overcome a serious drinking problem.

things still on the tables, pans of milk moulding in the dairies. . . . Forlorn dogs roamed around deserted homes, their doleful howls adding to the general sense of desolation."

"The enemy are laughing you to scorn. You must fight them. You must retreat no farther. The country expects you to fight. The salvation of the country depends on you doing so."

DAVID BURNET, PROVISIONAL PRESIDENT OF TEXAS, TO SAM HOUSTON

Years later, Texans would refer to Houston's retreat and this mass exodus humorously as the Runaway Scrape. For those involved, it was anything but funny. It was pure chaos that left the new government and its frail little army on the verge of complete collapse.

It was all so easy for Santa Anna, the "Napoleon of the West." He rode across Texas, Lieutenant de la Peña recalled, "with joy and in the highest spirits." And yet something very potent was brewing.

Historians have questioned the military value of Travis's stand at the Alamo. True, it resulted in heavy losses for Santa Anna. But Santa Anna rode out of Béxar on schedule with most of his army intact and ready for battle. Yet the "small affair" was still extremely important— it was a powerful symbol of free men trying to protect their homes, families, and land from a bloodthirsty tyrant.

Within days, newspapers throughout the United States were reporting the fall of the Alamo and Goliad and heaping abuse on Santa Anna and his troops. He was described as a "butcher" and a "bloody tiger"; his troops were labeled "vile scum . . . from the infernal regions."

Along with this rage came a call for immediate action. The citizens of many towns, especially those that had been the homes of Alamo

> HOUSTON'S MEN GREW ANGRY ABOUT THEIR CONSTANT RETREAT FROM THE ENEMY AND CAME VERY CLOSE TO FULL-SCALE MUTINY. AT ONE POINT, HOUSTON HAD NOTICES NAILED TO HICKORY TREES NEAR CAMP; THE NOTICES THREATENED TO HANG ANY MUTINEERS FROM THOSE TREES.

❧ THE ALAMO AFTER THE SIEGE ❧

When the Texas Rebellion ended, the Alamo was a shambles. Two battles had left the walls and buildings pockmarked and in ruins, and the Mexicans completed the job at the end of May as they left Béxar. "They are now as busy as bees," wrote eyewitness Dr. J. H. Bernard, "soldiers, convicts and all, tearing down the walls, etc. The Alamo was completely dismantled, all single walls were leveled, the fosse filled up, and the pickets torn up and burnt." After that, the abandoned mission-fort suffered further damage by the cold, rain, and blazing sun.

After the war, ownership of the complex passed through a number of hands, from the Catholic Church to the U.S. Army, private businesses, and the State of Texas. Very little was done to repair or restore the buildings during the nineteenth century, even though the legend of the Alamo and its brave defenders grew with each passing year. The U.S. Army did add windows and the unique "hump" on the front of the chapel in the 1840s, though many people, including Sergeant Edward Everett, condemned the new look: "Tasteless hands have evened off the rough walls . . . surmounting them with a ridiculous scroll, giving the building the appearance of the headboard of a bedstead."

Finally, the Daughters of the Republic of Texas, with the generous help of Clara Driscoll, purchased what was left of the

Two battles and years of neglect have left the Alamo chapel and adjoining wall in ruins in this 1848 watercolor by Seth Eastman.

Alamo in 1903 and set about repairing it. The grounds consist of 4.2 acres, but only the chapel and long barracks have survived. They seem curiously small these days, especially surrounded by the modern city of San Antonio that has grown up around them. Still, more than three million people visit the site every year, and many swear that the whispering sounds they hear are the ghostly voices of the Alamo defenders.

After the Alamo chapel was leased to the U.S. Army for a supply depot in the late 1840s, it was repaired and renovated. A second story was added, along with two windows and the structure's hump, seen in this watercolor by Robert Onderdonk.

The post–World War I photograph below shows what is left of the Alamo compound and how a busy, growing city is beginning to crowd in on it.

defenders, passed resolutions supporting independence for Texas and urging an invasion by U.S. forces. In Natchez, Mississippi, the citizens declared "that the proud dictator Santa Anna, like the fort Alamo, must fall. And the purple current of valiant gore that has moistened the plain in the cause of liberty must be avenged."

TEXAS

EXPECTS EVERY MAN TO DO HIS DUTY.

{ EXECUTIVE DEPARTMENT
of TEXAS.

FELLOW-CITIZENS OF TEXAS,

The enemy are upon us! A strong force surrounds the walls of San Antonio, and threaten that Garrison with the sword. Our country imperiously demands the service of every patriotic arm, and longer to continue in a state of *apathy* will be *criminal*. Citizens of Texas, descendants of Washington, awake! arouse yourselves!! The question is now to be decided, are we to continue as freemen, or bow beneath the rod of military despotism. Shall we, without a struggle, sacrifice our fortunes, our lives and our liberties, or shall we imitate the example of our forefathers, and hurl destruction upon the hands of our oppressors? The eyes of the world are upon us! All friends of liberty and of the rights of men, are anxious spectators of our conflict; or deeply enlisted in our cause. Shall we disappoint their hopes and expectations? No; let us at once fly to our arms, march to the battle field, meet the foe, and give renewed evidence to the world, that the arms of freemen, uplifted in defence of their rights and liberties, are irresistible. "Now is the day and now is the hour," that Texas expects every man to do his duty. Let us shew ourselves worthy to be free, *and we shall be free.* Our brethren of the United States have, with a generosity and a devotion to liberty, unparalleled in the annals of men, offered us every assistance. We have arms, ammunition, clothing and provisions; all we have to do, is to sustain ourselves for the present. Rest assured that

succors will reach us,' and that the people of the United States will not permit the chains of slavery to be rivetted on us.

Fellow-Citizens, your garrison at San Antonio is surrounded by more than twenty times their numbers. Will you see them perish by the hands of a mercenary soldiery, without an effort for their relief? They cannot sustain the seige more than thirty days; for the sake of humanity, before that time give them succor. Citizens of the east, your brethren of the Brazos and Colorado, expect your assistance, afford it, and check the march of the enemy and suffer not your own land to become the seat of war; without your immediate aid we cannot sustain the war. Fellow-citizens, I call upon you as your executive officer to "turn out;" it is your country that demands your help. He who longer slumbers on the volcano, must be a madman. He who refuses to aid his country in this, her hour of peril and danger is a traitor. All persons able to bear arms in Texas are called on to rendezvous at the town of Gonzales, with the least possible delay armed and equipped for battle. *Our rights and liberties must be protected*; to the battle field march and save the country. An approving world smiles upon us, the God of battles is on our side, and victory awaits us.

Confidently believing that your energies will be sufficient for the occasion, and that your efforts will be ultimately successful.

I subscribe myself your fellow-citizen,

HENRY SMITH,
Governor.

Elsewhere in the United States, troops were mobilized in response to the "small affair" and began moving toward Texas. Money was raised for arms and supplies.

The "small affair" roused the people of the United States and turned their attention toward Texas in a new way. The *New York Post* summed up the general feeling when it observed: "[Santa Anna] will shortly see that policy would have been required that he govern himself by the rules of civilized warfare. Had he treated the vanquished with moderation and generosity, it would have been difficult if not impossible to awaken that general sympathy for the people of Texas which now impels so many adventurous and ardent spirits to throng to the aid of their brethren."

Even those who did not favor an independent Texas were changed by the slaughter at the Alamo. "We have been opposed to the Texan war from the first to last," an editorial in the *Memphis Enquirer* confessed, "but our feelings we cannot suppress—some of our own bosom friends have fallen in the Alamo. We would avenge their death and spill the last drop of our blood upon the altar of Liberty."

The men and boys who had gone to Texas to acquire land and make their fortunes were remembered as defenders of liberty, much like their ancestors who had fought in the American Revolution. One Alamo defender, twenty-four-year-old Daniel Cloud, was eulogized in his hometown, Russellville, Kentucky, for "the many ties of friendship which he twined about our hearts" and for being a patriot who had "received the fatal shaft in the defense of liberty and humanity."

David Crockett's death seemed to touch everyone deeply. Most Americans would have agreed with the sentiments expressed by the *Natchez Courier* in Mississippi. After lamenting the deaths of Bowie, Travis, and all the other men, it concluded, "But there is something in the untimely end of the poor Tennessean that almost wrings a tear from us. It is too bad—by all that is good, it is too bad. The quaint, the laughter-moving, but the fearless upright Crockett, to be butchered by such a wretch as Santa Anna—it is not to be borne!"

While the nation mourned and mobilized, something just as important was taking place in the Texan Army. Even as Sam Houston had his troops backpedaling to avoid a direct clash with the onrushing Mexican Army, he was picking up more and more soldiers. The logic was simple and straightforward for the colonists: if they fled Texas, they would leave with absolutely nothing, not even their honor. If they surrendered, they would be put to death. The choice was obvious: stand and fight.

From 374 men on March 12, Houston's army would grow to nearly 1400 by the end of the month. Illness and desertion reduced his fighting force to a little more than 700 by mid-April, but Houston had an ally, one even he did not know about at the time. His name was Antonio López de Santa Anna.

Santa Anna, the fanatic about details, the student of Napoleon, had either overlooked or forgotten one of his hero's most important rules. "A general," Napoleon advised, "should say to himself many times a day: If the hostile army were to make its appearance on my front, on my right, on my left, what should I do?"

Quite simply, Santa Anna was still impatient with the speed of the campaign. So during the first week of April, he rushed ahead of the main columns of his army and most of his artillery, taking with him 750 men. To travel faster, he brought along only one brass cannon.

Sam Houston as he appeared in Martin J. Meade's 1846 painting.

"He is going with . . . inconceivable, rather astonishing haste. Why is His Excellency going in such haste? Why is he leaving the entire army behind? Does he think that his name alone is sufficient to overthrow the colonists?"

Lieutenant Colonel José Juan Sánchez Navarro in his diary

Before leaving, he ordered these men to leave behind every piece of equipment they did not absolutely need because his plan called for the utmost speed. He had received reports that the rebel government and Houston's army were nearby, and he wanted to capture and destroy them quickly and decisively. He was sure such a victory would end the rebellion. But he wanted to strike before the rebels got too close to the Mexican-U.S. border, where General Gaines waited with the Sixth

Regiment of the U.S. Army, hoping for some feeble excuse to take on Santa Anna.

Santa Anna's mad dash very nearly worked. At one point on April 15, fifty of his cavalry under the command of Colonel Juan Almonte had President Burnet and his entire cabinet within musket range. Burnet and the others were in a boat, desperately trying to row to safety across the San Jacinto River. They were easy targets, and the Mexicans were about to blast them out of the water when Almonte ordered them to put down their muskets. He had spotted Mrs. Burnet in the little boat and did not want to risk injuring her. And so these rebel ringleaders escaped because of an officer's deeply felt sense of honor.

Santa Anna's aide and interpreter, Colonel Juan Almonte.

Next, Santa Anna went after Houston and his army, who were reported to be only eight miles away. As he drove his troops onward, Santa Anna was fully aware that the bulk of his army—more than four thousand soldiers—was nowhere near, that in fact he was separating himself and his small force from it farther and farther every day. The problem for Santa Anna was that Sam Houston knew this too.

Scouts had been bringing Houston daily reports concerning the whereabouts of the Mexican Army. On the fifteenth, the day President Burnet and the rest of his revolutionary government barely escaped, Houston learned that the commander of the Mexican Army was actually in front of him, and far away from his reinforcements and supplies.

Houston acted swiftly. He turned his army east and positioned it so that Santa Anna and his small force were completely cut off from the main part of the Mexican Army. Houston and Santa Anna finally met near the San Jacinto River on April 20. Santa Anna hoped to lure Houston and his army into open battle, where the better-trained Mexican soldiers would have an advantage.

Santa Anna's one cannon opened fire, and a small force of soldiers advanced on the rebel line. The Texans responded with cannon fire of their own and a barrage of rifle fire that drove the Mexicans back. More cannon fire followed, and more rifle fire. But Houston refused to be drawn into the fight; instead, he withdrew his men to an area thick with giant oak and magnolia trees and surrounded on three sides by swamp.

At first glance this seemed like a terrible place for the Texas Army to hole up because there was no place to retreat to. But Santa Anna's next move turned the Texans' withdrawal into a strategic coup. As he saw Houston's men pulling back, the commander was so confident he held the better position that he did not call for an all-out charge, an offensive that many military scholars believe might have routed the Texans. Instead, Santa Anna hastily withdrew as well, to a spot four thousand feet from the Texans, and camped for the night near Peggy Lake.

As night fell, the situation became obvious to both commanders. Because of their superior rifles and marksmanship, the Texan Army now controlled the terrain in front of Santa Anna's army; behind the Mexicans lay deep water. Except for one bridge, Santa Anna and his troops were cut off, and everyone knew it. One of his own officers, Colonel Pedro Delgado, surveyed the situation and confided in his diary: "The camping ground of His Excellency was, in all respects, against military rules. Any youngster would have done better."

Santa Anna braced for an attack all night and throughout the morning of the twenty-first. But the Texans did not charge. General Cós arrived with four hundred reinforcements, and still the Texans made no move. The Mexican troops and their officers had lunch, then settled down for a well-deserved if ill-advised nap.

Three-quarters of a mile of flat prairie separated the two armies, a

THE TEXAN ARMY WENT INTO THE BATTLE OF SAN JACINTO LISTENING TO A FIFE AND DRUM PLAYING THE RISQUÉ TUNE "WILL YOU COME TO THE BOWER I HAVE SHADED FOR YOU."

The Battle of San Jacinto as painted by Henry Arthur McArdle.

stretch of open territory that no sensible soldier would cross during daylight. At least, that is what Santa Anna must have reasoned. For as his army drifted off to sleep, he failed to set out even one sentry to watch for the enemy's approach.

While they slept, Sam Houston acted.

First, Houston sent Erastus "Deaf" Smith and a handful of men to destroy Vince's Bridge, cutting off the only escape route for Santa Anna. Then Houston assembled his men and marched them across the prairie in three columns, with cavalry flanking them to the left near the river. No alarm was sounded from the Mexican side.

Next, the rebel army fanned out sideways, creating a line two men deep and almost a thousand feet long. Two pieces of artillery, known as the Twin Sisters, were hauled along in the center of the advancing troops. Houston rode his white horse, Saracen, across the front line of his men, urging them to hold their fire, encouraging them. "Victory is certain!" he shouted to his men. "Trust in God and fear not! And remember the Alamo, remember the Alamo!"

And remember they did. When they were six hundred feet from the enemy, the Twin Sisters were turned around and fired, sending a shower of razor-sharp metal into the sleeping Mexican camp. The Texan Army charged forward, almost immediately losing all sense of military discipline, breaking ranks in a mad dash to get at the enemy.

"We were all firing as rapidly as we could," recalled Private Alfonso Steele. "And as soon as we fired every man went to reloading, and he who first got his gun reloaded moved on, not waiting for orders. . . . When the second volley was poured into them . . . they broke and ran."

"Old Jimmie Curtice had a son-in-law, Wash Cottle, slain at the Alamo, whom he swore to avenge. The boys said he clubbed his rifle and sailed in, in Donnybrook fair style, accompanying each blow with 'Alamo! You killed Wash Cottle!' "

NOAH SMITHWICK IN *THE EVOLUTION OF A STATE, OR RECOLLECTIONS OF OLD TEXAS DAYS*

Houston had two horses shot out from under him, and his ankle was shattered by a musket ball, but he mounted a third horse and continued to lead the charge into the Mexican camp. Some Mexican soldiers attempted to put up a defense against the onrushing rebels, but there were too few of them to be much of an obstacle.

A Mexican colonel leaped onto ammunition crates to yell out commands to his men, but it was no use. "The utmost confusion prevailed," Colonel Delgado remembered. "General Castrillón shouted on one side; on another, Colonel Almonte was giving orders; some cried out to commence firing; others, to lie down and avoid grapeshot. Among the latter was His Excellency.

"Then, already, I saw our men flying in small groups, terrified, and sheltering themselves behind large trees. . . . They were a bewildered and panic-stricken herd."

After the opening volley, Santa Anna made an immediate decision. He hopped on another officer's horse and galloped away from the battle.

The Mexican soldiers meanwhile began throwing down their guns and running, only to discover there was no place to go. The soggy bayou and deep water of Peggy Lake slowed the terrified and mostly unarmed soldiers and made them easy targets.

The Mexicans pleaded for their lives, and a number of Texan officers

Charles Shaw aptly titled his painting Massacre at Peggy's Lake.

tried to stop the slaughter, but to no avail. Even Sam Houston's repeated orders to show mercy were ignored. "We obeyed no command but the impulse of our own feelings," wrote Robert Hunter. "We came, we saw, we conquered."

According to Houston, the Battle of San Jacinto—from the first shot to the capture of the Mexican camp—lasted just eighteen minutes. The slaughter that followed lasted several hours, with the furious cry of "Remember the Alamo!" echoing again and again and again. In the end, 9 Texans were killed and 34 wounded; 630 Mexicans were killed and 200 wounded. Those who survived—a little over 300 men—were captured and herded into the Texan camp.

One of those imprisoned was Santa Anna.

Some of Sam Houston's troops wanted Santa Anna to pay with his life for what had happened at the Alamo and Goliad. But Houston knew that Santa Anna was much more valuable to him alive. More than twenty-five hundred Mexican troops were now massed just two days away, with another thousand not far behind. Houston's far smaller army was exhausted, and no match should the remainder of the Mexican Army choose to attack.

So a bargain was struck. Santa Anna and what remained of his troops would be allowed to live if he ordered his entire army to leave Texas. The order was sent, and after a heated debate among the remaining generals, the Mexican Army withdrew across the Rio Grande. Immediately, the frightened refugees did an about-face and returned to what was left of their homes and towns—which were now part of an independent Texas Republic.

News of the defeat of the Mexican Army and the capture of Santa Anna reached a stunned Mexico City more than a week later. Minister of War José María Tornel grasped the importance of the

> SANTA ANNA WAS AT FIRST NOT RECOGNIZED BY HIS TEXAN GUARDS BECAUSE HE WAS WEARING A COMMON SOLDIER'S UNIFORM. HIS IDENTITY WAS REVEALED WHEN MEXICAN TROOPS SPOTTED HIM AND BEGAN SHOUTING, *"¡EL PRESIDENTE! EL PRESIDENTE!"*

> ONE OF THE FIRST THINGS SANTA ANNA DID AFTER SURRENDERING WAS TO ASK SAM HOUSTON FOR OPIUM. HE ASKED THE RIGHT MAN, SINCE HOUSTON WAS ALSO AN OPIUM USER.

event immediately. "The loss of Texas will inevitably result in the loss of New Mexico and the Californias," he predicted sadly. "Little by little our territory will be absorbed, until only an insignificant part is left us.... Our national existence ... would end like those weak meteors which, from time to time, shine fitfully in the firmament and disappear."

His prediction proved accurate. Under Santa Anna's leadership, which lasted on and off until 1855, Mexico lost more than 40 percent of its territory to the United States.

Sam Houston (stretched out on blanket with wounded leg) discusses surrender terms with Santa Anna (center, in white pants) in William Henry Huddle's painting.

The first official flag of the Republic of Texas, designed by Lorenzo de Zavala. It had a blue background and a single gold star in the center.

ANDREW JACKSON WAS RIGHT. AFTER THE UNITED STATES ANNEXED TEXAS IN 1846, THE MEXICAN-AMERICAN WAR BROKE OUT. THE UNITED STATES PROVED VICTORIOUS IN 1848.

Meanwhile, the Republic of Texas held its first election in September 1836, and Texans declared their desire to be annexed to the United States. But President Andrew Jackson and most of Congress were afraid such an action might result in full-scale war with Mexico and its European allies. Texas remained a separate country for ten years, with Mexican troops poised just across the border, ready to take possession once again. Finally, on February 19, 1846, the Lone Star flag of the Texas republic that hung at the capitol in Austin was lowered for the last time. The United States had finally added Texas to the Union.

By this time, the story of the Alamo and its brave defenders had grown into a formidable myth, lacing fact with speculation layered with distortion and outright fabrication. Today, professional and amateur historians pore over the available data and debate the many questions and riddles of the Alamo. How many Texans, Texian and Tejano, were actually in the Alamo on the final day? Did Travis really draw a line in the dirt? What illness did Bowie have, and was he alive when the Mexicans scaled the walls? Did Crockett die fighting or did he surrender and plead for mercy? How many Mexicans were killed?

The discussions and arguments will go on for generations, and the history of the Alamo will be refined and adjusted as new material emerges. But the aura surrounding the memory of the men who fought and died at the Alamo will remain untarnished.

Just three weeks after the Alamo's fall, the *Telegraph and Texas Register* understood that the sacrifice of those men had made them more than mere heroes. "We shall never cease to celebrate it. Spirits of the mighty, though fallen! Honors and rest are with ye: the spark of immortality which animated your forms, shall brighten into a flame, and Texas, the whole world, shall hail ye like the demi-Gods of old, as founders of new actions, and as patterns of imitation!"

"You ask me if I remember it. I tell you yes. It is burned into my brain and indelibly seared there. Neither age nor infirmity could make me forget, for the scene was one of such horror that it could never be forgotten by any one who witnessed the incidents."

ENRIQUE ESPARZA IN A 1907 NEWSPAPER ACCOUNT

Robert Maxham's recent view of the Alamo chapel. Every year approximately three million people walk through its doors and step into another era.

THOSE INSIDE THE ALAMO

The following is a list of those who are known to have been inside the Alamo at some time during the siege. At least 183 men died in the defense of the Alamo. In addition to these, I have also included the couriers who brought out Travis's messages, plus all of the women and children known to have been inside the Alamo.

* indicates a survivor   † indicates a courier   Ω indicates a child

Juan Abamillo
James L. Allen*†
Robert Allen
Juana Navarro de Alsbury*
Miles DeForest Andross
Micajah Autry
Juan Antonio Badillo
Peter James Baily III
Isaac G. Baker
William Charles M. Baker
John J. Ballentine
John J. Baugh
Joseph Bayliss
John Walker Baylor, Jr.*†
John Blair
Samuel Blair
William Blazeby
James Butler Bonham
David Bourne
James Bowie
Jesse B. Bowman
George Brown
James Brown
Robert Brown*†
James Buchanan
Samuel E. Burns
George D. Butler
John Cain
Robert Campbell
Madame Candelaria*
William R. Carey
Maria de Jesus Castro*Ω
Charles Henry Clark

M. B. Clark
Daniel W. Cloud
Robert E. Cochran
George Washington Cottle
Henry Courtman
Lemuel Crawford
David Crockett
Robert Crossman
Antonio Cruz y Arocha*
David P. Cummings
Robert Cunningham
Jacob C. Darst
John Davis
Freeman H. K. Day
Jerry C. Day
Squire Daymon
William Dearduff
Alexandro de la Garza*†
Stephen Dennison
Francis L. DeSauque*†
Charles Despallier
Lewis Dewall
Almeron Dickinson
Angelina Dickinson*Ω
Susannah Dickinson*
John Henry Dillard
Philip Dimitt*
James R. Dimpkins
Lewis Duel
Andrew Duvalt
Carlos Espalier
Ana Salazar Esparza*
Enrique Esparza*Ω

Francisco Esparza*Ω
Gregorio Esparza
Manuel Esparza*Ω
Robert Evans
Samuel B. Evans
James L. Ewing
William Keener Fauntleroy
William Fishbaugh
John Flanders
Dolphin Ward Floyd
John Hubbard Forsyth
Antonio Fuentes
Galba Fuqua
William Garnett
James W. Garrand
James Girard Garrett
John E. Garvin
John E. Gaston
James George
Petra Gonzales*
John C. Goodrich
Albert Calvin Grimes
Brigido Guerrero*
James C. Gwynne
James Hannum
John Harris
Andrew Jackson Harrison
William B. Harrison
Joseph M. Hawkins
John M. Hays
Charles M. Heiskell
Patrick Henry Herndon
William Daniel Hersee

Benjamin Franklin Highsmith*†
Tapley Holland
Samuel Holloway
William D. Howell
Thomas Jackson
William Daniel Jackson
Green B. Jameson
Gordon C. Jennings
Joe (Travis's slave)*
John
Lewis Johnson
William Johnson
William P. Johnson*†
John Jones
John Benjamin Kellog
James Kenney
Andrew Kent
Joseph Kerr
George C. Kimball
William Philip King
William Irvine Lewis
William J. Lightfoot
Jonathan L. Lindley
William Linn
Byrd Lockhart*
Concepción Losoya*
Juan LosoyaΩ
Toribio Losoya
George Washington Main
William T. Malone
William Marshall
Albert Martin
Mary (possibly slave of Jim Bowie)
Edward McCafferty
Jesse McCoy
William McDowell
James McGee
John McGregor
Robert McKinney
Eliel Melton
Juana Melton*
Thomas R. Miller

William Mills
Isaac Millsaps
Edward F. Mitchasson
Edwin T. Mitchell
Napoleon B. Mitchell
Robert B. Moore
Willis A. Moore
Robert Musselman
Andres Nava
Gertrudis Navarro*
George Neggan
Andrew M. Nelson
Edward Nelson
George Nelson
Benjamin F. Nobles
James Northcross
James Nowlan
William Sanders Oury*†
George Pagan
Christopher Adams Parker
William Parks
William Hester Patton*†
Alejo Perez, Jr.*Ω
Richardson Perry
Amos Pollard
John Purdy Reynolds
Thomas H. Roberts
James Waters Robertson
James M. Rose
Louis "Moses" Rose*
Jackson J. Rusk
Joseph Rutherford
Isaac Ryan
Trinidad Saucedo*Ω
Mial Scurlock
Juan Nepomuceno Seguín*†
Marcus L. Sewell
Manson Shied
Cleveland Kinloch Simmons
Andrew S. Smith
Charles S. Smith
John William Smith*†

Joshua G. Smith
William H. Smith
Launcelot Smither*†
Andrew Jackson Sowell*
Richard Starr
James E. Stewart
Richard L. Stockton
A. Spain Summerlin
William E. Summers
John Sutherland*†
William dePriest Sutherland
Edward Taylor
George Taylor
James Taylor
William Taylor
B. Archer M. Thomas
Henry Thomas
Jesse W. Thompson
John M. Thurston
Burke Trammel
William Barret Travis
George W. Tumlinson
James Tylee
Asa Walker
Jacob Walker
William B. Ward
Henry Warnell*
Joseph G. Washington
Thomas Waters
William Wells
Isaac White
Robert White
Hiram James Williamson
William Wills
David L. Wilson
John Wilson
Anthony Wolfe
———— WolfeΩ
———— WolfeΩ
Claiborne Wright
Damacio Xmenes
Charles Zanco

NOTES AND BIBLIOGRAPHY

Once you've read a few books about the Alamo, you will discover that the fight hasn't really ended yet. In 1836, the fight was about land and Texas independence. Nowadays, it is over what *really* happened back then. Yes, we know a great deal about the siege and final battle of the Alamo, but numerous questions remain: Exactly how many Alamo defenders were there? Did David Crockett die fighting or did he surrender, only to be executed? Did Travis draw a line in the dirt? How many Mexican soldiers were killed? Did Madame Candelaria care for Jim Bowie or was she a complete fraud? What flags flew during the siege?

These and many other questions are scrutinized and debated in books, in magazine articles, and on the Internet, and the exchanges can become heated. Historian Walter Lord tells about the time *The Columbia Encyclopedia* suggested that Crockett might very well have surrendered. The outcry over this entry from publications such as *Southwestern Historical Quarterly* was so strong and so angry that the encyclopedia's editors changed the text in the next edition. Whatever else can be said about the Alamo, it's clear that it is an extremely emotional subject for professional and amateur historians alike.

Most of these questions will probably never be answered definitively. New details will emerge as letters and journals come to light; existing documents will be retranslated and studied, and a slightly different interpretation of events will be put forward. This is not a situation unique to the Alamo. Almost every historical event and the people involved can be looked at in a variety of ways. The Alamo simply has an unusually high number of such unresolved issues.

What follows is a list of interesting and informative books and articles used to prepare my manuscript. Read just a few of these and you will be transported back to a time when our nation was young and raw and only beginning to take on the shape and character we know today.

Alsbury, Juana. "Mrs. Alsbury's recollections of the Alamo." An interview in the John S. Ford Papers, pp. 122–124. Center for American History, University of Texas at Austin. Juana Alsbury was Jim Bowie's cousin, and married to a Texian soldier who was away from Béxar when the Mexican army arrived. She never disputed that Madame Candelaria was in the Alamo, though she never actually saw her.

Barr, Alwyn. *Texans in Revolt: The Battle for San Antonio, 1835.* Austin: University of Texas Press, 1991. A detailed look at the issues and events that led to the first siege of the Alamo in 1835.

Baugh, Virgil E. *Rendezvous at the Alamo: Highlights in the Lives of Bowie, Crockett, and Travis.* Lincoln: University of Nebraska Press, 1960. A biography of the three main players inside the Alamo and how they came to be there in 1835. Includes sections on Jim Bowie's famed knife and various myths that have grown up around the siege and battle.

Burke, James Wakefield. *David Crockett: The Man Behind the Myth.* Austin: Eakin Press, 1984. Strips away the romantic image of Crockett to reveal a bright but uneducated man who managed to achieve a great deal more than anyone—including Crockett himself—could have imagined.

Candelaria, Andrea Castañon de Villanueva. In *The San Antonio Express*, March 6, 1892. Candelaria's account of her experiences during the siege. While many dispute that she was in the Alamo, much of what she says has a ring of authenticity.

Castañeda, Carlos E. *The Mexican Side of the Texas Revolution (1836) by the Chief Mexican Participants.* Austin: Graphic

Ideas, Inc., 1970. Originally published in 1928, this collection contains accounts by Generals Santa Anna, Filisola, and Urrea, along with those of Santa Anna's secretary, Ramón Caro, and Mexico's secretary of war, José María Tornel.

Chariton, Wallace O. *100 Days in Texas: The Alamo Letters.* Plano, TX: Wordware Publishing, Inc., 1990. A look at the Alamo siege and battle from December 9, 1835, through March 17, 1836, using letters, military dispatches, diary entries, and other firsthand accounts from those inside the Alamo, various Mexican officers, and many other leaders of the Texas Revolution.

Chemerka, William R. *Alamo Almanac & Book of Lists.* Austin: Eakin Press, 1997. An A to Z of people, places, and things associated with the Alamo, including the titles of many books and movies and how they have portrayed the deaths of Bowie and Crockett. The section of various Alamo-related lists contains several on who was and wasn't an Alamo defender.

Connelly, Thomas Lawrence. "Did David Crockett Surrender at the Alamo?" *Journal of Southern History* 26, no. 3 (August 1960): 368–76. Disputes the contention that Crockett gave up.

Crawford, Ann Fears, ed. *The Eagle: The Autobiography of Santa Anna.* Austin: State House Press, 1988. Santa Anna tells about his military career and service to his country and explains his actions at the Alamo. He claims to have been misunderstood and betrayed by his officers.

Crockett, David. *A Narrative of the Life of Col. David Crockett of Tennessee.* Boston: Allen & Ticknor, 1834. Crockett tells about his childhood and his many adventures. While he was not above exaggerating and posturing, this will let readers hear a master storyteller's voice.

Curilla, Richard. "The Degüello." *Alamo Lore and Myth Organization* 3, no. 3 (September 1981). A history of the song and why it was used at the Alamo.

Davis, William C. *Three Roads to the Alamo: The Lives and Fortunes of David Crockett, James Bowie, and William Barret Travis.* New York: Harper Collins, 1998. A biography of the three main characters inside the Alamo that presents them as flawed human beings who nevertheless managed to do something heroic.

de la Peña, José Enrique. *With Santa Anna in Texas: A Personal Narrative of the Revolution.* College Station, TX: Texas A&M University Press, 1975. We know de la Peña was with Santa Anna during the siege and served heroically during the final battle. We also know he wrote about his military career. But did he really write this narrative? We won't know the answer until the paper the narrative is written on is tested and the handwriting compared to verified samples of de la Peña's own handwriting.

DePalo, William A., Jr. *The Mexican National Army, 1822–1852.* College Station, TX: Texas A&M University Press, 1997. A scholarly study of the fighting units and weapons that Santa Anna brought north to fight the Texas Revolution.

Diaz, Pablo. Account in the *San Antonio Express*, July 1, 1906. Diaz was a teenager at the time of the siege and refused to serve in Seguín's company, a decision he later regretted. He watched the siege from the roof of the Mission Concepción.

Dickinson, Susannah. "Statement of Mrs. S. A. Hannig, wife of Almeron Dickinson." Adjutant General's Miscellaneous Papers, Texas State Library and Archives Commission, Austin. Also: "Testimony of Mrs. Hannig touching the Alamo Massacre. September 23, 1876." Texas State Library and Archives Commission, Austin. In addition, there are two accounts of the siege and battle by Dickinson in the *San Antonio Express*, April 28, 1881, and February 24, 1929. Susannah Dickinson brought news of the Alamo's fall to Sam Houston and would be dubbed the Messenger from the Alamo.

Elfer, Maurice. *Madame Candelaria: Unsung Heroine of the Alamo.* Houston: Rein Company, 1933. Brushes aside criticism of Candelaria to present a glowing picture of her actions in the Alamo.

Esparza, Enrique. "The Story of the Massacre of the Heroes of the Alamo." In the *San Antonio Express*, March 7, 1905. Esparza also has accounts in the *San Antonio Light*, November 10, 1901, and the *San Antonio Express*, May 12 and 19, 1907. Esparza's recollections are vivid and dramatic.

Filisola, Vicente. *Memoirs for the History of the War in Texas*, vol. I. Translated by Wallace Woolsey. Austin: Eakin Press, 1985. Santa Anna's second-in-command while in Texas has harsh views about the motives and honesty of Texian settlers and explains why he followed his commander's orders to retreat after the defeat at San Jacinto.

Foreman, Gary L. *Crockett, Gentleman from the Cane: A Comprehensive View of the Folkhero Americans Thought They Knew.* Dallas: Taylor Publishing, 1986. The myth and reality of Crockett are explored in detail.

Foster, William C. *Spanish Expeditions into Texas 1689–1768*. Austin: University of Texas Press, 1995. Describes the devilish Texas climate and terrain encountered by numerous expeditions and shows that Native American tribes had well-established trade routes and vital cultures.

Groneman, Bill. *Alamo Defenders: A Genealogy: The People and Their Words*. Austin: Eakin Press, 1990. Mini-biographies of everyone inside the Alamo during the siege. Also has numerous letters from Alamo defenders.

Groneman, Bill. "The Controversial Account of José Enrique de la Peña." A talk delivered at the 99th Annual Meeting of the Texas State Historical Association, San Antonio, March 1995. Groneman doesn't believe de la Peña's narrative is authentic.

Groneman, Bill. "Some Problems with the Almonte Account." *The Alamo Journal*, February 1994. Groneman examines a firsthand account by this Mexican officer and details various inconsistencies and errors.

Harburn, Dr. Todd E., D.O. "The Crockett Death Controversy: A Commentary and Opinion Regarding the Same As Contained in *Duel of Eagles, The Mexican and U.S. Fight for the Alamo*." *The Alamo Journal*, April 1991. An argument against Jeff Long's assertion that Crockett gave up and pleaded with Santa Anna for his life.

Hardin, Stephen L. *Texian Iliad: A Military History of the Texas Revolution, 1835–1836*. Austin: University of Texas Press, 1994. A detailed, fascinating discussion of the military aspects of the conflict.

Harrigan, Stephen. *The Gates of the Alamo*. New York: Alfred A. Knopf, 2000. A novel about an old man who tells of his involvement in the siege of the Alamo and how he managed to survive. Rich in atmosphere and characterization.

Hopewell, Clifford. *James Bowie: Texas Fighting Man: A Biography*. Austin: Eakin Press, 1994. A somewhat romantic view of Bowie's early years and exploits.

Hoyt, Edwin P. *The Alamo: An Illustrated History*. Dallas: Taylor Publishing, 1999. A straightforward discussion of the siege and battle accompanied by many pictures and maps.

Huffines, Alan C. *Blood of Noble Men: The Alamo Siege & Battle: An Illustrated Chronology*. Austin: Eakin Press, 1999. Begins on day one of the siege and ends with the final battle, mostly through firsthand accounts. Contains many realistic and accurate illustrations by Gary S. Zaboly.

Jackson, Jack. *Los Tejanos: The True Story of Juan N. Seguín and the Texas-Mexicans During the Rising of the Lone Star*.

Stamford, CT: Fantagraphics Books, Inc., 1982. An examination of how Tejano activities and support for the revolution were vital to Texas independence.

Kilgore, Dan. *How Did Davy Die?* College Station, TX: Texas A&M University Press, 1978. A look at the controversy surrounding Crockett's death.

King, Richard. *Susanna Dickinson, Messenger of the Alamo*. Austin: Shoal Creek Publishers, 1976. A full biography of Dickinson.

Lindley, Thomas Ricks. "A Correct List of Alamo Patriots." *The Alamo Journal*, December 1993. The author presents information suggesting that many more Texians were inside the Alamo than previously believed (as many as 250); he also suggests names of men who should be dropped from the list of Alamo defenders.

Lofaro, Michael A. *David Crockett: The Man, The Legend, The Legacy (1786–1986)*. Knoxville: University of Tennessee Press, 1985. A look at how Crockett was viewed before and just after his death at the Alamo and how his legend has evolved over the years.

Long, Jeff. *Duel of Eagles: The Mexican and U.S. Fight for the Alamo*. New York: William Morrow & Company, 1990. A well-documented and highly controversial history of the siege and final battle, plus a discussion of the involvement of the United States government in the Texas Revolution. Paints dark, unflattering pictures of Travis, Bowie, Crockett, and almost everyone else involved in the fight for Texas freedom.

Lord, Walter. *A Time to Stand: The Epic of the Alamo*. Lincoln: University of Nebraska Press, 1978. A stirring and detailed account of the growing troubles between Texians and the Mexican government, plus a day-by-day look at the siege and final battle. Includes a concise discussion of a variety of Alamo myths and controversies.

Lozano, Ruben Rendon. *Viva Tejas: The Story of the Tejanos, The Mexican-born Patriots of the Texas Revolution*. San Antonio: The Alamo Press, 1985. Brings to light many of the things Tejanos did to help defeat Santa Anna and achieve Texas independence.

Lundstrom, John B. "Assault at Dawn: The Mexican Army at the Alamo." *The Magazine of Military History*, No. 1 (Summer 1973). A detailed discussion of troops under Santa Anna's command.

Lyman, Rick. "Mexican's Memoir of Alamo a Rage: Story of Davy Crockett's Execution Is Going on Auction Block."

The New York Times, November 18, 1998. An article about the pending auction of de la Peña's diary that focuses on the passionate debate about the authenticity of the text.

Mahoney, Bob. "Flags of the Alamo." *The Alamo Journal*, December 1986. A discussion of the two flags known to have been there, and others that may have been.

Matovina, Timothy M. *The Alamo Remembered: Tejano Accounts and Perspectives*. Austin: University of Texas Press, 1995. A collection of Tejano voices, gathered to present their side of the siege and revolution.

McDonald, Archie P. *Travis*. Austin: Jenkins Publishing Company, 1976. Presents the nice and nasty sides of Travis's personality.

Millsaps, Isaac. Letter from the Alamo. In the Daughters of the Republic of Texas Library at the Alamo. Some historians question the authenticity of this letter, but its tone and words paint a dramatic picture of life at the Alamo during the siege.

Myers, John Myers. *The Alamo*. Lincoln: University of Nebraska Press, 1948. An interesting discussion of Mexico's failure to colonize Texas with its own people and how this eventually led to conflict between Texians and the Mexican government. Detailed description of the Alamo mission, along with sections on Travis, Bowie, Crockett, and Santa Anna.

Nackman, Mark E. *A Nation Within a Nation: The Rise of Texas Nationalism*. Port Washington, NY: Kennikat Press, 1975. Contains a look at Texian relations with Mexico before the revolution of 1836.

Nelson, George. *The Alamo: An Illustrated History*. Dry Frio Canyon, TX: Aldine Press, 1998. Contains numerous maps as well as illustrations.

Nosworthy, Brent. *With Musket, Cannon and Sword: Battle Tactics of Napoleon and His Enemies*. New York: Sarpedon, 1996. A look at the way Napoleon used troops and the weapons of war to battle enemies, and how they countered his moves.

Petite, Mary Deborah. *1836 Facts About the Alamo & the Texas War for Independence*. Mason City, IA: Savas Publishing, 1999. Many facts about many subjects, including a chronology of the Texas War for Independence, a summary of Tejano revolutionaries, biographies of both Texan and Mexican officers at the Alamo, and much more.

Pohl, James W. *The Battle of San Jacinto*. Austin: Texas State Historical Association, 1989. A detailed look at the military strategies of Houston and Santa Anna and the ensuing battle.

Proctor, Ben H. *The Battle of the Alamo*. Austin: Texas State Historical Association, 1986. A concise history of the siege and battle.

Ragsdale, Crystal Sasse. *Women & Children of the Alamo*. Austin: State House Press, 1994. The only book to focus exclusively on this group and their activities inside the Alamo.

Sánchez Navarro, Lt. Col. José Juan A. "A Mexican View of the Texas War: Memoirs of a Veteran of the Two Battles of the Alamo." *The Library Chronicle* of the University of Texas at Austin IV, no. 2 (Summer 1951). Navarro was an officer under General Cós and was very angry about the December loss of the Alamo to the Texians, whom he considered inferior in every way.

Schoelwer, Susan Pendergast, with Tom W. Glaser. *Alamo Images: Changing Perceptions of a Texas Experience*. Dallas: DeGolyer Library and Southern Methodist University Press, 1985. A collection of most of the important depictions of the battle and the characters involved and a discussion of how they have changed over the years as the Alamo myth has evolved.

de la Teja, Jesús F., ed. *A Revolution Remembered: The Memoirs and Selected Correspondence of Juan N. Seguín*. Austin: State House Press, 1991. One of Texas's greatest patriots tells his story of the siege and battle and discusses how he and other Tejanos were maligned and stripped of their holdings after the war.

Tinkle, Lon. *13 Days to Glory: The Siege of the Alamo*. College Station, TX: Texas A&M University Press, 1996. Though somewhat fictionalized, overall this is a stirring "you are there" account of the last days of the Alamo garrison.

Todish, Tim J., and Terry S. Todish. *Alamo Sourcebook 1836: A Comprehensive Guide to the Alamo and the Texas Revolution*. Austin: Eakin Press, 1998. This sourcebook covers a wide range of subjects, from a technical look at the weapons used, to biographies of the participants, to a day-to-day weather log and much, much more.

INDEX

ABOUT THE AUTHOR

Jim Murphy became interested in the siege of the Alamo after a friend asked him if it was true that Davy Crockett had escaped capture by passing himself off as a woman, complete with dress and wig. "It turned out to be one of the many bogus stories that have surfaced about David Crockett," Murphy says, "but it started me thinking about how the reality, myth, and make-believe of the Alamo and those involved have often been mixed together and presented as history. It was out of this fascination that the idea developed for this inside look at the siege."

An award-winning author of more than twenty-five books, Jim Murphy has twice received SCBWI's Golden Kite Award and NCTE's Orbis Pictus Award for nonfiction. In addition, his *The Great Fire* was a Newbery Honor Book, and his *Blizzard! The Storm That Changed America* was a Robert F. Sibert Informational Book Award Honor Book.

Jim Murphy lives in Maplewood, New Jersey, with his wife, Alison, and their two sons, Michael and Ben.